PASTA
EVERY WAY FOR EVERY DAY

CONTENTS

INTRODUCTION

The Italians, who are masters at combining sophistication with simplicity, have eaten pasta over the past millennium. They know that no other food can nourish and delight so easily, while asking for so small an effort on the part of the cook. Simple yet sustaining, a dish of pasta satisfies our hunger yet invites the eye and pleases the palate with its countless shapes, colours and flavours. It is the most versatile of foods, changing its character with ease, according to season, occasion, cook's mood or time available.

In this book we concentrate mainly on dried pasta, which is the pasta that the Italians eat religiously and lovingly every day of every week. It is the pasta they always have on hand, and it is the pasta that pairs most successfully with the greatest number of different sauces.

Some of the sauces we have chosen are classic, others are modern and many are variations on a traditional theme. There are slow-simmered sauces that can be prepared totally ahead of time, as well as many quick-fix sauces that can be made just before eating, so a whole meal can be put together in half an hour or less. Put together, yes, but always with love, care and attention.

When the family is ready to eat, the pasta slides into a pan full of boiling water, and the cook shouts *Ho messo giù la pasta* - I've put the pasta in. A few minutes later everyone sits down in silence and the cook brings in the bowl of steaming pasta and sets it in the middle of the table for people to serve themselves. Pasta is a convivial, sharing food; to our mind, it is best not formally plated.

We leave the last word to the actor Alberto Sordi in the wonderful movie *A Taxi Driver in America* -

Dove c'è pasta, c'è speranza.

Where there's pasta, there's hope.

Anna Enric

Notes From the Cooks

BEFORE YOU COOK read through the recipe carefully. Make sure you have all the equipment and ingredients required.

On Cooking Times

Always take cooking times as guideline rather than gospel. In each recipe, we qualify estimated cooking times with a description of how the ingredient should look at the end of cooking time, for instance "cook until soft, 5 minutes". It is better to cook the ingredient until its appearance matches the given description rather than simply setting the stopwatch.

Various factors affect cooking times, with your choice of pan and the character of your oven at the top of the list.

The size and shape of a pan directly affect how quickly a dish will cook. The same sauce cooked over the same heat will cook faster in a wide, shallow pan and more slowly in a tall, deep pot. The larger cooking surface of a wide pan ensures rapid evaporation, while the high sides of deep pots will inhibit evaporation. In each recipe, we have specified the size and shape of pan required for a quick cook or slow cook sauce.

Ovens vary from kitchen to kitchen. Most have hot spots, so be prepared to rotate dishes from top to bottom or from front to back during cooking time. An oven thermometer is a useful kitchen tool, allowing you to match your oven's temperature with the one specified in the recipe. Always allow a margin of 5-10 minutes either way for baking times.

On Tasting

Always taste food as you cook and before you serve. Don't be afraid to add or change flavours to suit your palate – the fun of cooking is in experimenting, improvising, creating. Ingredients differ from day to day, season to season and kitchen to kitchen. Be prepared to adjust sweetness, sharpness, spiciness, and, most important of all, salt, to your own taste.

On Salt and Pepper

Discerning seasoning makes the difference between good and great food. As a general rule, seasoning is best done towards the end of cooking. The optimum moment for a cook to judge how much salt and pepper a recipe requires is at the end of cooking time, when the flavours have blended.

On Measuring

Accurate measurements are essential if you want the same good results each time you follow a recipe. We have given measurements in metric and imperial in all the recipes. Always stick to one set of measurements. Never use both in the same recipe.

Kitchen scales are the most accurate way to measure dry ingredients. We recommend using scales for all except the smallest amounts.

We also recommend using cooks' measuring spoons when following a recipe. All spoon measurements in the book are level unless otherwise stated. To measure dry ingredients with a spoon, scoop the ingredient lightly from the storage container, then level the surface with the edge of a straight-bladed knife.

We use standard level spoon measurements:
    1 tbsp - 15ml (½ floz)
    1 tsp - 5ml (⅙ floz)

To measure liquids, choose a transparent glass or plastic measuring jug. Always place the jug on a flat surface and check for accuracy at eye level when pouring in a liquid to measure.

A final and important rule of measuring - never measure ingredients over the mixing bowl!

THE TEN COMMANDMENTS

Pasta is everyday food, yet any Italian knows that the cooking and serving of it calls for care and attention. Remember these ten golden rules for perfectly cooked pasta every time.

- Buy good quality Italian pasta.

- Use a large pot full of water.

- Salt the water with a generous hand.

- Boil the water and keep it boiling.

- Stir the pasta often - it will stick if you don't!

- Start timing when the water returns to the boil.

- Don't wander off! As they say in Italy, *gli spaghetti amano la compagnia* - spaghetti loves company.

- Drain immediately, but not too thoroughly.

- Have the sauce and a warmed bowl ready.

- Eat up! The only time people stop talking in Italy is when a bowl of pasta is placed on the table.

PASTA IN THE KITCHEN

The key to making perfect pasta is to start with the right pot. When cooking 500g (1lb) dried pasta, the pot should hold about 5 litres (8½ pts) of water to give the pasta plenty of room to move around.

A pot made of an inexpensive, lightweight metal like aluminium is ideal, since it conducts heat evenly and is easy to lift when full of boiling water. A stockpot will also make a good pasta pot, as it is usually taller than it is wide and has two sturdy handles for lifting.

A large colander is also essential. A colander has the advantage over a sieve in that the water drains more slowly, which will prevent the cooked pasta from becoming a sticky mass. Choose a colander with feet so that the base stands well above the cooking water when it is emptied into the kitchen sink.

The type of pan used to cook a pasta sauce will directly affect the required cooking time and character of the

finished sauce. The larger cooking surface of a wide frying pan ensures rapid evaporation, which is essential for a quick-cook sauce.

A heavy-based, deep pot is best for a slow-cooked sauce. The high sides guard against over-evaporation and the heavy base prevents sticking when a long simmering time is required.

1 Tall, narrow, lightweight pasta pot with a lid

2 Long-handled wooden spoon for stirring pasta

3 Large colander with feet

4 Large frying pan for quick-cook sauces

5 Heavy-based pot with a lid for slow-cook sauces

PASTA AT THE TABLE

In an Italian home, pasta is always served from a large bowl set in the middle of the table. A wide bowl with shallow sloping sides is traditional. If the bowl is too deep the high sides will inhibit the tossing, and therefore the proper saucing, of the pasta. As soon as the pasta and its sauce are together, they must be tossed immediately. A large fork and spoon, or two forks, do the job best.

Pasta is a simple food. The success of a pasta dish will owe much to the quality of its ingredients. In Italy, freshly ground black pepper and freshly grated cheese are basic necessities, making a cheese grater and a pepper grinder essential equipment, both in the kitchen and at the table.

1. Large bowl for tossing and serving
2. Large fork and spoon for tossing
3. Pepper grinder
4. Cheese grater
5. Oven-proof baking dish

WHICH PASTA?

WHAT IS GOOD PASTA?

There is only one important rule to remember when buying pasta. Good ingredients are essential for good pasta.

• Choose pasta made from one hundred per cent durum wheat. Always check that the packet reads either *pasta di semola di grano duro* or durum wheat pasta. Durum wheat is a hard wheat grain - in fact the hardest wheat grown. Pasta made with durum wheat will maintain its shape, texture and flavour while cooking in rapidly boiling water.

• Choose pasta made in Italy wherever possible. In Italy, both the composition and the manufacture of dried pasta are tightly controlled by law. Pasta produced in other countries can be made from ordinary soft wheat flours or from blends with durum wheat. When cooked, pasta made from inferior types of flour will have a limp, sometimes gluey, texture as well as a tendency to overcook easily.

PLAIN OR EGG?

Dried pasta divides into two types: pale yellow plain pasta made with durum wheat and water, and golden yellow egg pasta made with durum wheat and whole eggs. Egg pasta has a smoother, silkier texture; plain pasta has a firm, chewy bite. Neither is superior to the other - they are simply different. In Italy, it is the sauce that determines the choice between dried plain pasta and dried egg pasta. Oil-based sauces are usually served with plain pasta and butter-based and cream-based sauces with egg pasta.

FRESH OR DRY?

We still come across the widespread misconception that fresher is better. This is not so. Truly fresh pasta that is worth buying is made with good quality flour and real eggs and no other additives. Finding this can present a challenge. We will always choose a quality boxed dried pasta imported from Italy over a pre-packaged fresh pasta from the supermarket.

Homemade fresh egg pasta is another story. The finest fresh pasta is always made at home, using the best ingredients. Turn to pages 144-145 if you have the time and the enthusiasm to learn how.

WHICH SAUCE?

There are said to be six hundred different pasta shapes in Italy. Of these, about fifty are the common shapes that are easily found. But, since different regions of Italy and different manufacturers sometimes give different names to the same shape, there is often confusion. So, when pairing pasta with sauce, it is best not to focus on all the different shapes of pasta. Think instead about the pasta sauce - its consistency and texture - and which pasta it would coat and complement best. As a general rule, slippery or more delicate sauces are best paired with long pasta strands or ribbons. Short pasta shapes and tubes suit thicker or chunkier sauces that cling to the hollows of the pasta and get caught inside the holes. But remember, cooking and eating pasta is no different from all cooking and eating; whatever venerable traditions and classical rules there may be, always trust your own palate. At the end of the day, it's a matter of personal choice.

LONG PASTA - STRANDS & RIBBONS

Long and thin dried pasta ribbons and strands should be dressed with light, oil-based sauces which allow the strands to remain separate and slippery. Strands and ribbons that are thicker, such as bucatini or tagliatelle, are best when paired with sauces based on cream, cheese and eggs, or with sauces based on meat. Dried egg pasta ribbons, such as fettuccine and pappardelle, also pair well with these same types of sauces. A good guideline for matching long pasta to sauce is whether the sauce ingredients will cling to the pasta when it is twirled on a fork.

1. Pappardelle - *Broad egg ribbons*
2. Tagliolini - *Very thin egg ribbons*
3. Fettuccine - *Thin egg ribbons*
4. Tagliatelle - *Medium egg ribbons*
5. Bucatini - *Thick hollow strands*
6. Linguine - *"Little Tongues"* - *Thin ribbons*
7. Spaghettini - *"Little Spaghetti"* - *Very thin strands*
8. Spaghetti - *Thin strands*
9. Capellini - *"Angel's Hair"* - *Very fine strands*

SHORT PASTA - TUBES & SHAPES

When matching short pasta to sauce, be sure that the size of the pasta complements the size of the sauce ingredients. The chunkier the ingredients in the sauce, the larger the hollow or cup required to capture them. This is an important guideline to follow in order to allow a balanced mouthful of sauce and pasta to be enjoyed when the finished dish is eaten. Pasta tubes and shells come in many different sizes. Large pasta tubes and shells are excellent paired with rich meat sauces or robust vegetable sauces, or used in baked dishes. Medium-sized short pasta tubes, shells or shapes go well with vegetable sauces and are also good for pasta salads.

1 Orecchiette - *"Little Ears"- Medium disk-shaped shells*

2 Conchiglie - *Shell-shaped pasta, available in different sizes*

3 Gnocchetti - *"Little Dumplings" - Ridged shell-shaped pasta*

4 Chifferi - *Elbow-shaped tubes, available ridged and smooth*

5 Penne - *"Quills" - Diagonally cut tubes, available smooth or ridged and in different sizes*

6 Rigatoni - *Large ridged tubes*

HOW MUCH PASTA?

There is no rigid rule about how much pasta to cook. It all depends on whom you are feeding and what else you are feeding them.

A traditional meal in Italy has no "main" course, it is rather a succession of harmonious courses of which pasta is usually one. Outside Italy, pasta is generally served as the main event, making a complete meal in itself when paired with a crusty loaf of bread and a fresh green salad.

A good rule of thumb is to allow about 75g (2½ oz) of pasta for a first course serving and 125g (4oz) for a main course serving. The recipes in this book will generally serve about six people as a starter and four people as a main course.

THE SALT

The addition of salt to the pasta cooking water is an essential step that must not be omitted. When pasta is cooked in unsalted water, no matter how flavourful the sauce, the dressed pasta will be certain to have a bland taste.

• Use a coarse grain or flaked salt with no additives. Coarse or flaked salt will dissolve more quickly than a fine grain salt.

• We always use coarse grain or flaked sea salt. The quality of salt does matter, as different salts have different flavours and levels of saltiness.

• Add salt to the boiling water 1 to 2 minutes before the pasta to give the salt time to dissolve.

• When cooking 500g (1lb) dried pasta, add about 1½ tbsp coarse grain salt to 4 to 5 litres (6 to 8 pints) of boiling water.

THE OIL MYTH

If you use the correct amount of water, add the pasta when the water is boiling rapidly, and remember to stir the pasta immediately, the addition of olive oil becomes totally unnecessary. It is in fact a waste of olive oil.

THE BOIL

WHEN TO ADD IT?

When the water is salted and boiling, slide in the pasta all at once. All the pasta must be added at the same time to ensure that it cooks uniformly.

Stir immediately with a long wooden fork or spoon to prevent the pasta from sticking to the bottom of the pot. During cooking, stir occasionally to keep the pasta in constant motion.

HOW LONG TO COOK IT?

Always start timing from the moment the water returns to a rapid, rolling boil after the pasta has been added to the pot. The actual cooking time will depend on the quality, size and shape of the pasta. Use the timings printed on the packet only as a guide. The way to know when the pasta is cooked is to take some out and have a bite. We advise you to begin testing about 2 minutes before the packet instructions suggest it should be done.

THE BITE

IS IT DONE?

As with all cooking and eating, the ideal point of doneness is always a matter of personal taste. As a general rule, pasta is perfectly cooked when it is tender but still retains some resistance - meaning you should still feel its texture when you bite into it. *Al dente* literally translates as "to the tooth", but "to the bite" is probably a more useful description.

IS IT UNDERCOOKED?

The pasta will still have a chalky core and a slight taste of raw flour.

IS IT OVERCOOKED?

The pasta will have lost all its springy and chewy qualities.

COOKING FRESH PASTA

Uncooked fresh pasta is heavier because it contains more moisture than dried. Allow about 125g (4oz) for a first course serving, 150g (5oz) for a main course serving.

Don't skimp on the cooking water. The right proportion of water to pasta is even more critical in the case of fresh pasta.

Fresh pasta cooks in very little time, so make sure that the sauce is ready and the bowl warm before you slide the pasta into the water. Once the water returns to the boil, begin testing for doneness after 1 minute.

THE DRAIN

When the pasta is done, it must be drained immediately. Every second the pasta remains in the hot water it will continue to cook.

• Be ready. Have your colander in the sink. As soon as the pasta is firm to the bite, tip it from the pot into the colander and give the colander two or three sharp shakes.

• Don't overdrain. Draining pasta properly is important. Pasta should never be overdrained. It should remain slippery so that it can be properly coated with the sauce. How well-drained the pasta should be depends on the type of pasta and its shape.

• Long pasta strands or ribbons should be left still lightly dripping with water.

• Short pasta tubes or shapes should be drained more thoroughly as their hollows and holes will hold more water.

• Fresh egg pasta needs the least thorough draining. It should remain very slippery with water after draining as it will tend to absorb more of the sauce than a plain dried pasta.

BEFORE YOU DRAIN

When the recipe specifies, we suggest that you remove about half a cupful of the pasta water from the pot and set it aside just before draining. Use the reserved water to adjust the consistency of the finished dish when it is needed. If the pasta is overdrained, if the sauce is too thick, or if the sauced pasta is too dry, add a few tablespoons of the reserved pasta water. Using the pasta water is always preferred to adding hot water from the tap as the cooking water contains the pasta starch and salt. This adds both body and seasoning as well as moisture to the finished pasta dish.

THE TOSS

Speed is essential when saucing, tossing and serving pasta. Have everything you need on hand. Make sure your family or guests are gathered at the table and ready to eat.

• Don't delay! Sauce the pasta as soon as it has been drained. Pasta should never be allowed to sit in the colander without any sauce. Always have the sauce hot, ready, and waiting.

• Sauce the pasta in a warmed serving bowl or in the still-warm pasta cooking pot. Even better is to add the pasta straight to the sauce in the pan. Tossing everything together in the pan in which the sauce was cooked provides a warm surface to ensure the pasta blends perfectly with the sauce.

• Use two large forks, or a large fork and a spoon, to toss the pasta. Mix well, until every strand or piece of pasta is lightly and evenly coated with the sauce. If the pasta seems dry, drizzle in a little of the reserved pasta cooking water (see box opposite). The starch in the water helps the sauce to cling to the pasta and to coat every surface as uniformly as possible.

• Don't oversauce. The sauce should moisten, not drown, the pasta. It's not only the sauce that gives flavour to a pasta dish. The pasta has a taste and character of its own. You want the taste of the pasta as well as the sauce to come through.

• Pasta cools quickly, so have warmed serving dishes ready. Place an oven-proof serving bowl and/or individual plates in a 120°C (250°F) Gas ½ oven to warm through while you cook the pasta. Or, just before serving, place in the sink and pour over hot water.

CHEESE
Always use fresh Italian Parmesan and always grate it freshly just before using. Grated Parmesan, however, is not an essential accompaniment to each and every pasta dish. In Italy, it is certainly never added indiscriminately. Parmesan is traditionally associated with richer and creamier sauces. Its addition would be considered heresy in many shellfish dishes, and it is even considered an optional extra on many olive-oil-based vegetable and tomato sauces.

THE RECIPES

PASTA WITH TOMATOES

TOMATOES IN THE PASTA PANTRY

Tinned tomatoes are an essential pantry basic to be kept on hand at all times. Always choose tinned tomatoes over unripe and out of season fresh tomatoes – even if it means changing your menu accordingly. There's no need to discard any leftover tinned tomatoes not required in the recipe; tinned tomatoes in their juice refrigerate and freeze well.

A quick and easy way to chop up whole tinned tomatoes is to use kitchen scissors to chop them while they are still in the tin. When making a slow-simmered tomato sauce, you can add the tomatoes whole from the tin and break them up in the pan with a wooden spoon.

Tomato purée is best bought in a tube as it keeps well in the refrigerator and can be used a spoonful at a time. If you have opened a tin, you can freeze any leftover tomato purée not required in the recipe. Simply freeze the remaining purée in the tin and, when it has frozen solid, open the base of the tin with a tin opener and push out the block of purée. You can then cut it into slices, put it back in the freezer, and use each slice as needed.

Although jars of sun-dried tomatoes in oil are a handy pantry item, demi-sec sun-dried tomatoes have a superior flavour. Seek them out in gourmet stores and from mail order sources (see page 167). If buying loose, make sure they are still chewy and not too dry. To soak, place in a bowl with 1 tbsp red wine vinegar, pour over boiling water to cover and leave to stand until tender and swollen.

Choose fresh tomatoes that are firm, red and at their seasonal best. Plum tomatoes are the ideal variety for pasta sauces as their flesh is thick and meaty. When flavour is a priority, however, ripeness is more important than variety. When cooking with fresh tomatoes outside their peak season, it's well worth thinking ahead and buying the tomatoes a few days in advance of using. Set them on a tray by the kitchen window, making sure they are not touching, and leave for a few days to ripen. Never store tomatoes in the refrigerator; chilling gives the tomato flesh a pappy texture.

Taking the extra time and care to peel fresh tomatoes will make for a finished dish with a superior texture, flavour and appearance. However, when time is at a premium, it is a step that can be skipped. See page 156 for how to peel and seed fresh tomatoes.

NO COOK
RED PESTO

SERVES 4

60g (2 oz) sun-dried tomatoes in oil, drained
2 garlic cloves, crushed
2½ tbsp pine nuts, toasted
½ tsp crushed chilli flakes
5 tbsp extra virgin olive oil
½ - 2 tsp balsamic vinegar
black pepper
500g (1lb) dried pasta

Place tomatoes, garlic, pine nuts, chilli flakes and oil in a food processor; pulse to a smooth paste. Add vinegar and pepper to taste. Set aside or store, see below. Cook pasta in a large pot of boiling, salted water, until firm to the bite if serving hot, or just firm to the bite if serving as a salad. Drain, reserving ½ cup pasta water. Return pasta with pesto to the warm pasta pot. Toss well to coat, adding reserved water as needed. Serve immediately or at room temperature.

WHICH PASTA?
Strands or shapes - spaghettini, spaghetti, penne.

THINK AHEAD
Make pesto up to 4 days in advance. Cover and refrigerate. If serving as a salad, dress pasta up to 8 hours ahead. Cover and store at room temperature.

VARIATIONS
RED PESTO WITH ROCKET
Add 2 handfuls rocket leaves with the pesto and the drained pasta to the warm pasta pot. Finish as directed.

RED PESTO WITH BASIL
Add 1 handful torn fresh basil with the pesto and the drained pasta to the warm pasta pot. Finish as directed.

NO COOK
FRESH TOMATO

SERVES 4

500g (1lb) dried pasta
6-7 ripe tomatoes, seeded and diced
1 garlic clove, crushed
5 tbsp extra virgin olive oil
salt, black pepper

Cook pasta in a large pot of boiling, salted water, until firm to the bite if serving hot or just firm to the bite if serving as a salad. While pasta is cooking, combine tomatoes, garlic and oil. Add salt and pepper to taste. Let stand while pasta is cooking to allow the flavours to blend. Drain pasta. Toss drained pasta with marinated tomatoes in a large serving bowl. Serve warm or at room temperature.

WHICH PASTA?
Strands or thin ribbons - spaghetti, linguine.

THINK AHEAD
Make sauce up to 8 hours in advance. Cover and store at room temperature. If serving as a salad, dress pasta up to 8 hours in advance. Cover and store at room temperature.

VARIATIONS
FRESH TOMATO AND MOZZARELLA
Return drained pasta with tomatoes and 250g (8oz) diced mozzarella to warm pasta pot. Toss well to coat. Serve immediately.

FRESH TOMATO AND LEMON
Add 1 tbsp fresh lemon juice and ½ tsp grated lemon zest to the tomatoes. Finish as directed.

FRESH TOMATO, RED ONION AND BASIL
Add ½ finely sliced red onion and 1 handful torn fresh basil to the tomatoes. Finish as directed.

FRESH TOMATO AND OLIVES
Add 10 sliced pitted black olives to the tomatoes. Finish as directed.

FRESH TOMATO, ROCKET AND BALSAMIC VINEGAR
Add 2 tsp balsamic vinegar and 1 handful roughly chopped rocket to the tomatoes, garlic and olive oil. Finish as directed.

NO COOK
SUN-DRIED TOMATO WITH CHILLI, GARLIC AND BLACK OLIVES

SERVES 4

500g (1lb) dried pasta
12 sun-dried tomatoes in olive oil, drained and sliced
150g (5oz) pitted black olives, sliced
3 garlic cloves, finely chopped
½ tsp crushed chilli flakes
1 tsp red wine vinegar
6 tbsp extra virgin olive oil
1 tbsp chopped fresh basil or flat-leaf parsley
salt, black pepper

Cook pasta in a large pot of boiling, salted water, until firm to the bite if serving hot or just firm to the bite if serving as a salad. While pasta is cooking, combine tomatoes, olives, garlic, chilli, vinegar and oil. Drain pasta. Return pasta with basil or parsley and tomato mixture to the warm pasta pot. Toss well to coat. Add salt and pepper to taste. Serve immediately or at room temperature.

WHICH PASTA?
Strands or thin ribbons - spaghetti, linguine.

THINK AHEAD
Mix sauce ingredients up to 8 hours in advance. Cover and store at room temperature. If serving as a salad, dress pasta up to 8 hours in advance. Cover and store at room temperature.

QUICK COOK
PUTTANESCA
SERVES 4

500g (1lb) dried pasta
5 tbsp extra virgin olive oil
½ tsp crushed chilli flakes
2 garlic cloves, finely sliced
6 anchovy fillets, drained
  and chopped

2 - 400g (14oz) tins Italian
  plum tomatoes or 1kg (2lb)
  fresh tomatoes, chopped
150g (5oz) pitted black
  olives
1 tbsp capers, drained
salt, black pepper

Cook pasta in a large pot of boiling, salted water, until firm to the bite. While pasta is cooking, heat oil in a large frying pan. Add chilli flakes, garlic and anchovies. Cook, stirring constantly over medium heat, until anchovies have disintegrated, 2-3 minutes. Raise heat to medium high, add tomatoes and cook, stirring occasionally, until thickened, 15 minutes. Add olives and capers. Add salt and pepper to taste. Drain pasta. Add drained pasta to the hot sauce and toss well to coat. Serve immediately.

WHICH PASTA?
Strands or tubes - spaghetti, penne, rigatoni.

THINK AHEAD
Make sauce up to 3 days in advance. Cover and refrigerate.

COOKS' NOTE
The name derives from 'puttana' - prostitute. It allegedly originated in Trastevere, the haunt in Rome of these nocturnal ladies. And its name no doubt owes something to the fact that it is a piquant sauce, very quickly made.

QUICK COOK
NAPOLITANA

SERVES 4

500g (1lb) dried pasta
7 tbsp extra virgin olive oil
1 garlic clove, crushed
1kg (2lb) fresh ripe tomatoes,
  chopped or 2 - 400g (14oz) tin
  Italian plum tomatoes, chopped
1 tsp sugar
1 handful torn fresh basil
salt, black pepper

Cook pasta in a large pot of boiling, salted water until firm to the bite. While pasta is cooking, place oil, garlic, tomatoes, sugar and basil in a large frying pan on medium-high heat. Simmer rapidly until thickened, 10 minutes. Add salt and pepper to taste. Drain pasta. Add pasta to the hot sauce. Toss well to coat. Serve immediately.

WHICH PASTA?
Strands or tubes - spaghetti, penne, rigatoni.

THINK AHEAD
Make sauce up to 3 days in advance. Cover and refrigerate.

QUICK COOK
ARRABBIATA

SERVES 4

7 tbsp extra virgin olive oil
1 medium onion, finely sliced
3 garlic cloves, sliced
1 tsp crushed chilli flakes
2 - 400g (14oz) tins Italian plum
  tomatoes, chopped
salt, black pepper
500g (1lb) dried pasta
2 tbsp torn fresh basil or flat-leaf
  parsley, optional

Heat oil in a large frying pan. Add onion, garlic and chilli and cook, stirring frequently over medium high heat, until soft and golden, 7 minutes. Add tomatoes and cook, stirring occasionally, until thickened, 15 minutes. Add salt and pepper to taste. Meanwhile, cook pasta in a large pot of boiling, salted water until firm to the bite. Drain. Add pasta with your choice of herb, if using, to the hot sauce. Toss to coat. Serve immediately.

WHICH PASTA?
Strands or tubes - spaghetti, penne, rigatoni.

THINK AHEAD
Make sauce up to 3 days in advance. Cover and refrigerate.

COOKS' NOTE
The name of this sauce from Central Italy means 'angry', because of the potency of its flavour.

FRESH TOMATO SAUCE

SERVES 4

500g (1lb) dried pasta	**salt, black pepper**
6 tbsp extra virgin olive oil	**1 handful torn fresh basil**
3 garlic cloves, crushed	**leaves, optional**
750g (1½ lb) ripe fresh	**additional extra virgin**
tomatoes, peeled (optional)	**olive oil to toss**
and cut into 6 pieces	

Cook pasta in a large pot of boiling, salted water, until firm to the bite. While pasta is cooking, heat oil in a large frying pan. Add garlic and cook over medium heat until fragrant, 1 minute. Add tomatoes and cook, stirring frequently, until tomatoes are sizzling hot but still retaining their fresh flavour and bright colour, about 5 minutes. Add salt and pepper to taste. Drain pasta. Add pasta, with the basil if using, to the hot sauce. Toss well to coat, adding 2 tbsp additional olive oil as needed. Serve immediately.

WHICH PASTA?
Strands or thin to medium ribbons - spaghetti, fettuccine, tagliatelle.

VARIATIONS
FRESH TOMATO SAUCE WITH PESTO
Omit basil. Add 3 tbsp simple basil pesto (see page 105) with the drained pasta to the hot sauce.

FRESH TOMATO SAUCE WITH MOLTEN MOZZARELLA
Make sauce as directed. Turn down heat to low. Add 125g (4oz) diced mozzarella to sauce and heat gently until just melting, 1 minute. Omit the additional 2 tbsp olive oil. Finish as directed.

PIQUANT FRESH TOMATO SAUCE
Add 8 sliced pitted black olives, 2 tsp capers, rinsed and drained, and ¼ tsp crushed chilli flakes with the tomatoes to the pan. Finish as directed.

FRESH TOMATO SAUCE WITH RICOTTA
Make sauce as directed. Turn down heat to low. Add 125g (4oz) crumbled ricotta to sauce and heat gently until warm through, 1 minute. Omit the additional 2 tbsp olive oil. Finish as directed.

SPICY FRESH TOMATO SAUCE
Add ¼ tsp crushed chilli flakes with the garlic to the pan. Finish as directed.

SLOW COOK
TOMATO AND MOZZARELLA AL FORNO

SERVES 4

2 tbsp extra virgin olive oil
2 cloves garlic, crushed
2 - 400g (14oz) tins Italian plum tomatoes, chopped or
　1kg (2lb) fresh tomatoes, seeded and chopped
2 tsp fresh or 1 tsp dried oregano
salt, black pepper
500g (1lb) dried pasta
250g (8oz) mozzarella cheese, cut in to 2.5cm (1in) cubes
60g (2oz) freshly grated parmesan, plus additional
　to serve

Preheat oven to 200°C (400°F) Gas 6.
Heat oil in a large frying pan. Add garlic and cook over medium high heat until fragrant, 1 minute. Add tomatoes and oregano and simmer rapidly, stirring occasionally, until thickened, 15 minutes. Add salt and pepper to taste. Remove and reserve 6 tbsp tomato sauce from the pan. Meanwhile, cook pasta in a large pot of boiling, salted water, until just firm to the bite. Drain, reserving ½ cup pasta water. Toss drained pasta with remaining sauce, adding reserved water as needed. Place half the pasta in an oiled 30cm x 20cm x 5cm (12in x 8in x 3in) oven-proof dish. Cover with half the mozzarella and half the parmesan. Top with remaining pasta. Cover with reserved tomato sauce and remaining mozzarella. Sprinkle with remaining parmesan. Bake until golden and bubbling, 15 minutes.

WHICH PASTA?
Tubes or shapes - penne, rigatoni, fusilli.

THINK AHEAD
Assemble and leave to cool completely. Cover unbaked and refrigerate up to 8 hours in advance. Bake as directed. Alternatively, cover unbaked and freeze up to 3 weeks in advance. Defrost overnight in refrigerator. Cook in preheated 200°C (400°F) Gas 6 oven for 30 minutes.

VARIATION
PAN-COOKED TOMATO AND MOZZARELLA
Make sauce as directed, but over low heat add mozzarella to the hot sauce and heat gently until just melting, 1 minute. Meanwhile, cook pasta in a large pot of boiling, salted water, until firm to the bite. Drain, reserving ½ cup pasta water. Add drained pasta with parmesan to the hot sauce. Toss well to coat, adding reserved water as needed. Serve hot with extra parmesan.

SLOW COOK
ROAST TOMATO

SERVES 4

6 fresh ripe tomatoes, halved
2 garlic cloves, crushed
¼ tsp crushed chilli flakes
½ tsp dried oregano
salt, black pepper
3 tbsp extra virgin olive oil
2 tbsp balsamic vinegar
500g (1lb) dried pasta
2 tbsp freshly grated parmesan,
  plus additional to serve
additional extra virgin olive oil

Preheat oven to 150°C (300°F) Gas 2.
Place tomato halves cut side up in an
oven tray. Sprinkle with garlic, chilli
flakes, oregano, salt and pepper. Drizzle
over oil and vinegar. Roast in oven
until very soft and wilted, 1½ hours.
Meanwhile, cook pasta in a large pot
of boiling, salted water, until firm to
the bite. Drain. Place drained pasta in
a warm bowl and toss with parmesan
and 1-2 tbsp additional extra virgin
olive oil. Place tomatoes on top. Serve
immediately with additional parmesan.

WHICH PASTA?
Strands or ribbons – spaghetti, linguine, fettuccine,
tagliatelle, pappardelle.

THINK AHEAD
Roast tomatoes up to 1 day in advance. Cover
and refrigerate. Reheat in preheated 200°C (400°F)
Gas 6 oven for 10 minutes.

VARIATIONS
ROAST TOMATO WITH PESTO
Add 4 tbsp simple basil pesto (see page
105) in place of the parmesan and oil to
the drained pasta.

ROAST TOMATO WITH RICOTTA AND BASIL
Add 125g (4oz) crumbled ricotta and
1 handful torn basil with the parmesan
to the drained pasta.

ROAST TOMATO WITH CRISPY PANCETTA
Cook 4 unsmoked pancetta or
unsmoked streaky bacon slices, turning
frequently, in a large frying pan over
medium low heat until browned and
crisp, 10 minutes. Drain on paper
towels and cut into strips 2.5cm (1in)
wide. Add pancetta with the parmesan
to the drained pasta.

SLOW COOK
SIMMERED TOMATO

SERVES 4

4 tbsp extra virgin olive oil
1 medium onion, finely chopped
1 garlic clove, crushed
2 - 400g (14oz) tin plum tomatoes, chopped
salt, black pepper
500g (1lb) dried pasta
freshly grated parmesan to serve, optional

Place oil, onion, garlic and tomatoes in a heavy based pot.
Bring to a fast simmer over medium heat. Turn heat to low and
simmer gently, stirring occasionally, until thick and deep red,
30-40 minutes. If the sauce becomes too dry and starts to stick,
add a few tablespoons of water. Add salt and pepper to taste.
Meanwhile, cook pasta in a large pot of boiling, salted water,
until firm to the bite. Drain. Add pasta to the hot sauce. Toss
well to coat. Serve immediately with parmesan.

WHICH PASTA?
Strands and tubes - spaghettini, spaghetti, penne, rigatoni.

THINK AHEAD
Make up to 3 days in advance. Cover and refrigerate. If making variations with
cream, add cream just before serving.

VARIATIONS
SIMMERED TOMATO WITH RED WINE AND ROSEMARY
Add 125ml (4floz) red wine and 2 tsp finely chopped fresh
rosemary with the onion, garlic and tomatoes to the pot.
Cook and serve as directed.

SIMMERED TOMATO WITH AROMATICS
Add 1 finely chopped celery stalk and 1 finely chopped small
carrot with the onion, garlic and tomatoes to the pan. Cook
and serve as directed.

SIMMERED TOMATO WITH CINNAMON AND BAY
Add ¼ tsp cinnamon and 5 dry or 10 fresh bay leaves with the
onion, garlic and tomatoes to the pan. Cook and serve as
directed, removing the bay leaves before serving.

SIMMERED TOMATO WITH CREAM
Omit oil. Cook sauce as directed. Transfer to food processor;
pulse until smooth. Return to pan over medium heat. Stir in
125ml (4floz) double cream and cook until hot through,
1-2 minutes. Serve as directed.

SIMMERED TOMATO WITH VODKA
Omit oil. Cook sauce as directed. Transfer to food processor;
pulse until smooth. Return to pan over medium heat. Add 3 tbsp
vodka and simmer rapidly to evaporate alcohol, 2 minutes. Stir
in 125ml (4floz) double cream and 30g (1oz) butter and cook
until hot through, 1-2 minutes. Serve as directed.

PASTA WITH BUTTER AND CHEESE

CHEESE IN THE PASTA PANTRY

No pasta lover's pantry is complete without a wedge of Parmesan in the refrigerator. Always buy Parmesan in a piece, never pre-grated. It's best to buy a wedge that weighs no more than 250g-300g (8-10oz), as a larger piece will probably dry out before you use it up. Store wrapped in foil in the warmest part of the refrigerator. If it does dry out, try wrapping it in a piece of damp muslin to re-moisten. Parmesan can be frozen and it will retain its flavour well, but it will become too crumbly to grate when defrosted.

We always buy Italian Parmesan and, whenever possible, *Parmigiano Reggiano*. Although more expensive, it is unquestionably superior in flavour and texture. We like to present Parmesan at the table in a manageable piece with a small hand grater and allow everyone to enjoy freshly grating their own additional cheese. Otherwise, grate it first in the kitchen and serve it in a bowl.

Pecorino Romano is a tangy, salty sheep's milk cheese which is also suitable for grating. It is traditionally served with pasta dishes originating from southern Italy, where pungent flavours dominate. When called for in a recipe, it is because the distinctively sharp taste of Pecorino is the best complement to the sauce. And, although we do list grated Parmesan as an alternative, we urge you to seek out Pecorino cheese from Italian speciality and gourmet shops to serve when it is the appropriate choice for the recipe.

Gorgonzola is a creamy coloured, blue-veined cheese with a flavour that varies from mildly tangy to piquant. When buying Gorgonzola for pasta, remember that the creamier the consistency, the mellower the flavour.

When buying mozzarella at the supermarket, always choose whole milk "fresh" mozzarella that comes in a squashed, ball shape and is sold in plastic bags surrounded by water. Never buy the rubbery blocks of mozzarella. Real mozzarella is made from the milk of the Italian water buffalo and has a fresher flavour than mozzarella made from cow's milk. But, for cooking, the superior buffalo mozzarella is not essential.

NO COOK
BUTTER AND PARMESAN

SERVES 4

500g (1lb) dried pasta
125g (4oz) butter, cut into cubes
100g (3½oz) freshly grated parmesan
salt, black pepper
additional freshly grated parmesan, to serve

Cook pasta in a large pot of boiling, salted water, until firm to the bite. Drain. Return pasta to the warm pasta pot. Add butter to the pasta. Toss well to coat. Add parmesan and salt and pepper to taste. Serve immediately with additional parmesan.

WHICH PASTA?
Strands or ribbons - spaghetti, tagliolini, fettuccine, tagliatelle, pappardelle.

COOKS' NOTE
Don't hold back on the black pepper - this dish is best with generous amounts.

VARIATIONS
BUTTER, PARMESAN AND HAM
Add 4 slices ham, cut into short, fine strips, 2.5cm (1in) long and 0.5cm (¼in) wide, to pasta with butter. Finish as directed.

BUTTER, PARMESAN AND PARSLEY
Add 2 tbsp finely chopped fresh flat-leaf parsley to pasta with the butter. Finish as directed.

BUTTER, PARMESAN AND ASPARAGUS
Cook 250g (8oz) small asparagus tips in boiling, salted water until just tender, 2-3 minutes. Drain and add immediately to hot pasta with the butter. Toss gently to avoid crushing. Finish as directed.

BUTTER, PARMESAN AND PEAS
Cook 125g (4oz) tiny frozen peas in boiling, salted water until just tender, 2 minutes. Drain and add immediately to hot pasta with the butter. Finish as directed.

NO COOK
CREAM AND PARMESAN

SERVES 4
250ml (8floz) double cream
2 egg yolks, beaten
60g (2oz) freshly grated parmesan
500g (1lb) dried pasta
salt, black pepper
**additional freshly grated parmesan
  to serve**

Mix cream, egg yolks and parmesan in a
bowl until combined. Meanwhile, cook
pasta in a large pot of boiling, salted
water, until firm to the bite. Drain pasta,
reserving ½ cup pasta water. Return
pasta to the warm pasta pot. Add cream
mixture. Toss well to coat, adding
reserved water as needed. Add salt and
pepper to taste. Serve immediately with
additional parmesan.

WHICH PASTA?
Ribbons - fettuccine, tagliatelle, pappardelle.

NO COOK
THREE CHEESE

SERVES 4
500g (1lb) dried pasta
90g (3oz) freshly grated parmesan
90g (3oz) grated emmental, gruyère or edam
90g (3oz) grated mozzarella, fontina or provolone
125g (4oz) butter
black pepper

Cook pasta in a large pot of boiling, salted water, until firm to the bite. Drain,
reserving ½ cup pasta water. Return drained pasta with parmesan, your choice of
other cheeses and butter to the warm pasta pot. Toss well to coat, adding reserved
water as needed. Add pepper to taste. Serve immediately.

WHICH PASTA?
Medium tubes or shapes - penne, macaroni, fusilli, conchiglie.

NO COOK
GORGONZOLA AND RICOTTA

SERVES 4

500g (1lb) dried pasta
4 tbsp crumbled gorgonzola
125g (4oz) ricotta, crumbled
60g (2oz) butter
salt, black pepper
additional crumbled gorgonzola to serve

Cook pasta in a large pot of boiling, salted water, until firm to the bite. Drain, reserving ½ cup pasta water. Return pasta with gorgonzola, ricotta and butter to the warm pasta pot. Toss well to coat, adding reserved water as needed. Add salt and pepper to taste. Serve immediately, sprinkled with an additional 2 tbsp gorgonzola.

WHICH PASTA?
Medium tubes or shapes - ditali, penne, macaroni, fusilli, conchiglie.

VARIATIONS

GORGONZOLA, RICOTTA AND BABY SPINACH
Add 2 handfuls baby spinach leaves to the drained pasta with the gorgonzola and ricotta. Finish as directed.

GORGONZOLA, RICOTTA AND BASIL
Add 1 handful fresh basil leaves to the drained pasta with the gorgonzola and ricotta. Finish as directed.

GORGONZOLA, RICOTTA AND ROCKET
Add 2 handfuls rocket leaves to the drained pasta with the gorgonzola and ricotta. Finish as directed.

QUICK COOK
GORGONZOLA CREAM

SERVES 4

500g (1lb) dried pasta
30g (1oz) butter
125g (4oz) crumbled gorgonzola
3 tbsp milk
175ml (6floz) double cream
salt, black pepper

Cook pasta in a large pot of boiling, salted water, until firm to the bite. While pasta is cooking, melt butter in a large frying pan over low heat. Add gorgonzola and milk and warm gently, stirring constantly, until melted, 2 minutes. Stir in cream and warm gently until hot through, 1 minute. Add salt and pepper to taste. Drain pasta. Add pasta to the hot sauce. Toss well to coat. Serve immediately.

WHICH PASTA?
Ribbons - tagliolini, fettuccine, tagliatelle, pappardelle.

QUICK COOK
LEMON, BASIL AND MASCARPONE

SERVES 4

500g (1lb) dried pasta
5 tbsp lemon juice
1 tsp grated lemon zest
250g (8oz) mascarpone
salt, black pepper
1 handful torn fresh basil

Cook pasta in a large pot of boiling, salted water, until firm to the bite. While pasta is cooking, place lemon juice and zest and mascarpone in a large frying pan over medium-low heat. Warm gently, stirring constantly, until heated through, 3-4 minutes. Add salt and pepper to taste. Drain pasta, reserving ½ cup pasta water. Add pasta with basil to the hot sauce. Toss well to coat, adding reserved water as needed. Serve immediately.

WHICH PASTA?
Ribbons or strands - linguine, fettuccine, tagliatelle.

COOKS' NOTE
Mascarpone is an Italian cream cheese; here its richness is lightened by the lemon and the basil.

QUICK COOK
FOUR CHEESES AL FORNO

SERVES 4

500g (1lb) dried pasta
75g (2½ oz) butter
60g (2oz) gruyère, cut into
  1cm (½ in) cubes
60g (2oz) fontina, cut into
  1cm (½ in) cubes

100g (3½ oz) mozzarella, cut into
  1cm (½ in) cubes
6 tbsp freshly grated parmesan
pinch cayenne pepper
additional freshly grated
  parmesan to top
1 tbsp dried breadcrumbs

Preheat oven to 200°C (400°F) Gas 6.
Cook pasta in a large pot of boiling, salted water, until just firm to the bite. Drain, reserving ½ cup pasta water. Return pasta with butter to warm pasta pot and stir to coat. Add gruyère, fontina, mozzarella, parmesan and cayenne. Mix thoroughly until the cheese is melting but not completely melted, adding reserved water as needed. Place in a buttered 30cm x 20cm x 5cm (12in x 8in x 3in) oven-proof dish. Sprinkle with 1 tbsp additional parmesan and breadcrumbs. Bake until just golden and crusty, 10-15 minutes. Leave to stand for 5 minutes before serving.

WHICH PASTA?
Medium tubes or shapes - penne, macaroni, fusilli, conchiglie.

THINK AHEAD
Assemble up to 1 day in advance. Cover unbaked and refrigerate. Allow an extra 5 minutes in the oven when cooking from cold.

QUICK COOK
GOLDEN SAFFRON

SERVES 4

60g (2oz) butter
1 shallot, finely chopped
pinch saffron threads, soaked in
  4 tbsp boiling water
125ml (4floz) dry white wine
125ml (4floz) tbsp double cream
salt, black pepper
500g (1lb) dried pasta

Melt butter in a large frying pan over medium heat. Add shallot and cook, stirring frequently, until soft, 5 minutes. Add saffron, saffron water and wine and simmer rapidly until reduced by half, 5 minutes. Add cream and cook until thickened, 1 minute. Add salt and pepper to taste. Meanwhile, cook pasta in a large pot of boiling, salted water, until firm to the bite. Drain, reserving ½ cup pasta water. Add pasta to the hot sauce. Toss well to coat, adding reserved water as needed. Serve immediately.

WHICH PASTA?
Medium to wide ribbons - fettuccine, tagliatelle, pappardelle.

QUICK COOK
ALL'ALFREDO

SERVES 4

500g (1lb) dried pasta
30g (1oz) butter
250ml (8floz) double cream
salt, black pepper
60g (2oz) freshly grated parmesan
additional freshly grated parmesan
** to serve**

Cook pasta in a large pot of boiling, salted water, until firm to the bite. While pasta is cooking, place butter and cream in a large frying pan over medium-low heat. Heat through, then simmer gently until just thickened, 1-2 minutes. Add salt and pepper to taste. Drain pasta. Add parmesan and cooked pasta to the hot sauce. Toss well to coat. Serve immediately with additional parmesan.

WHICH PASTA?
Medium to wide ribbons - fettuccine, tagliatelle, pappardelle.

COOKS' NOTE
Fettuccine is the traditional pasta to serve with this famous sauce. Alfredo was the owner of a restaurant in Rome where the great and the good flocked in the 1950s and 60s. He used to give a final toss to the tagliatelle with a large gold fork and spoon before setting the dish on the tables.

Pasta with Mushrooms

MUSHROOMS IN THE PASTA PANTRY

The very best and most authentic mushrooms for pasta are the meaty textured, earthy flavoured porcini and boletus varieties, but cultivated brown and field mushrooms, especially if used in combination with dried porcini, are an acceptable and economical substitute. White button mushrooms, however, are not a suitable substitute. To boost and enhance the flavour of cultivated mushrooms, mix 15g (½ oz) of dried porcini with 250g (8oz) fresh mushrooms. Never wash fresh mushrooms under running water. To clean, use a damp cloth or piece of kitchen paper and wipe away any dirt.

When buying dried porcini, choose packets with the largest mushroom pieces, as they come from the caps. The smaller, crumbly bits are the dried stalks and have less flavour than the caps. Porcini should be reconstituted in hot water for a minimum of 30 minutes. Try this alternative method when making creamy mushroom sauces: place the porcini in a small pan with equal amounts of water and milk to cover. Bring to a boil and boil for 1 minute. Remove from heat and leave to soak for 20 minutes. Use the soaked mushrooms and flavourful milky soaking liquid in the sauce. Dried porcini will keep in a cool, dark place for up to 1 year.

QUICK COOK
WILD MUSHROOM PERSILLADE

SERVES 4

2 tbsp extra virgin olive oil
2 garlic cloves, finely chopped
2 shallots, finely chopped
500g (1lb) wild
  mushrooms, sliced
salt, black pepper
500g (1lb) dried pasta
4 tbsp freshly grated parmesan
3 tbsp finely chopped fresh
  flat-leaf parsley
additional freshly grated parmesan

Heat oil in a large frying pan. Add garlic and shallots and cook over medium-high heat until fragrant, 1 minute. Add mushrooms and cook, stirring frequently, until tender and coloured, 10 minutes. Add salt and pepper to taste. Meanwhile, cook pasta in a large pot of boiling, salted water, until firm to the bite. Drain, reserving ½ cup pasta water. Add pasta with parmesan and parsley to the hot mushrooms. Toss well to coat, adding reserved water as needed. Serve immediately with additional parmesan.

WHICH PASTA?
Strands or thin to medium ribbons - spaghetti, fettuccine, tagliatelle.

COOKS' NOTE
There are many varieties of wild mushrooms. You can use a single variety or a mixture for this recipe. Our preferred choice would be fresh porcini or chanterelles, but field mushrooms and chestnut mushrooms have a good rich flavour, are easy to find and inexpensive.

QUICK COOK
MUSHROOM, WHITE WINE AND CREAM

SERVES 4

500g (1lb) dried pasta
30g (1oz) butter
1 tbsp extra virgin olive oil
1 garlic clove, finely chopped
250g (8oz) brown or wild mushrooms
  (see page 56), finely sliced
4 tbsp white wine
125ml (4floz) double cream
salt, black pepper
freshly grated parmesan to serve

Cook pasta in a large pot of boiling, salted water, until firm to the bite. While pasta is cooking, melt butter with oil in a large frying pan over medium-high heat. Add garlic and mushrooms and cook, stirring frequently, until just coloured, 5 minutes. Add wine and simmer until just evaporated. Stir in cream and simmer gently until just thickened, 1-2 minutes. Drain pasta, reserving about ½ cup pasta water. Add pasta to the hot sauce. Toss well to coat, adding reserved water as needed. Serve immediately with parmesan.

WHICH PASTA?
Medium to wide ribbons - fettuccine, tagliatelle, pappardelle.

COOKS' NOTE
Use field or chestnut mushrooms for this dish if wild mushrooms are beyond the budget or not available. For a superlative dish with an even deeper mushroom flavour, we strongly recommend adding dried porcini mushrooms (see variation below).

VARIATION
PORCINI, WHITE WINE AND CREAM
Soak 25g (1oz) packet of dried porcini (see page 156). Finely chop and add to the hot pan with the garlic and fresh mushrooms. Cook as directed. Add the reserved mushroom-soaking liquid with the wine. Finish as directed.

QUICK COOK
TOMATOES WITH PORCINI

SERVES 4

25g (1oz) dried porcini mushrooms
30g (1oz) butter
3 tbsp extra virgin olive oil
1 small onion, finely chopped
1 garlic clove, finely chopped
1 – 400g (14oz) tin Italian plum tomatoes, chopped
500g (1lb) dried pasta
freshly grated parmesan to serve

Soak the dried porcini (see page 156). Drain, reserving the soaking liquid, and finely chop. Set aside.
Melt butter with olive oil in a large frying pan over medium heat. Add onion and garlic and cook until softened, 5 minutes. Add tomatoes and cook, stirring occasionally, until thickened, 10 minutes. Adjust heat to low. Add porcini mushrooms and reserved soaking liquid and simmer gently for 5 minutes. Meanwhile, cook pasta in a large pot of boiling, salted water, until firm to the bite. Drain. Add pasta to the hot sauce. Toss well to coat. Serve immediately with parmesan.

WHICH PASTA?
Strands, tubes or shapes - spaghetti, penne, fusilli.

THINK AHEAD
Make sauce up to 3 days in advance. Cover and refrigerate.

SLOW COOK
MUSHROOM AL FORNO

SERVES 4 - 6

25g (1oz) dried porcini mushrooms
1 tbsp extra virgin olive oil
30g (1oz) butter
250g (8oz) brown or wild mushrooms, finely sliced
1 tsp fresh or ½ tsp dried thyme
2 garlic cloves, crushed
500g (1lb) dried pasta
6 tbsp freshly grated parmesan

FOR BECHAMEL
75g (2½oz) butter
4½ tbsp flour
750ml (1¼ pints) milk
salt, black pepper, nutmeg

Soak the porcini (see page 156). Drain, reserving the soaking liquid, and finely chop. Set aside.
Preheat oven to 200°C (400°F) Gas 6.
For bechamel, melt butter over medium heat in a heavy saucepan. Whisk in flour and cook until foaming, about 1 minute. Remove from heat and gradually pour in milk, whisking constantly. Return to heat and cook, whisking constantly, until sauce thickens, about 2 minutes. Bring to the boil and remove from the heat. Add salt, pepper and nutmeg to taste. Stir in porcini mushrooms and reserved soaking liquid. In a small pan, melt butter with oil and add fresh mushrooms, thyme and garlic. Cook over medium-high heat, stirring frequently, until mushrooms are just coloured, 5 minutes. Remove from heat. Stir in to bechamel. Meanwhile, cook pasta in a large pot of boiling, salted water, until just firm to the bite. Drain. Combine drained pasta and mushroom bechamel. Add 2 tbsp of the parmesan. Toss. Place in a buttered 30cm x 20cm x 7.5cm (12in x 8in x 3in) oven-proof dish. Sprinkle the remaining parmesan over top. Bake until golden and bubbling, 10 minutes. Leave to stand for 5 minutes before serving.

WHICH PASTA?
Tubes or shells - penne, macaroni, rigatoni, conchiglie.

THINK AHEAD
Assemble and leave to cool completely. Cover, unbaked, and refrigerate up to 1 day in advance. Alternatively, freeze up to 3 weeks in advance. Defrost overnight in refrigerator. Cook in preheated 200°C (400°F) Gas 6 oven for 30 minutes.

PASTA WITH SEAFOOD

SMOKED SALMON, VODKA AND DILL

SERVES 4

500g (1lb) dried pasta
60g (2oz) butter
1 tsp vodka
125ml (4floz) sour cream
salt, black pepper
200g (7oz) smoked salmon,
  cut into strips
1 tbsp dill sprigs

Cook pasta in a large pot of boiling, salted water, until firm to the bite. Drain, reserving ½ cup pasta water. Return drained pasta to the warm pasta pot. Add butter, vodka and half the sour cream. Toss well to coat, adding reserved water as needed. Add salt and pepper to taste. Top with salmon, remaining sour cream and dill. Serve immediately.

WHICH PASTA?
Thin to medium ribbons - linguine, fettuccine, tagliatelle.

TUNA WITH LEMON AND CAPERS

SERVES 4

500g (1lb) dried pasta
2 – 200g (7oz) tins tuna in oil,
  drained and flaked
250g (8oz) cherry tomatoes
1 tbsp drained capers
handful fresh basil, torn
6 tbsp extra virgin olive oil
½ tsp lemon zest
2 tbsp lemon juice
salt, black pepper

Cook pasta in a large pot of boiling, salted water, until firm to the bite if serving hot or just firm to the bite if serving as a salad. Drain. Return drained pasta to the warm pasta pot. Add tuna, tomatoes, capers, basil, oil and lemon zest and juice. Toss well to coat. Add salt and pepper to taste. Serve immediately or at room temperature.

WHICH PASTA
Tubes or shells - conchiglie, gnocchi, rigatoni.

THINK AHEAD
Make up to 1 day in advance if serving as a pasta salad. Cover and refrigerate. Bring to room temperature before serving.

SALMON CAVIAR WITH BUTTER AND CHIVES

SERVES 4

500g (1lb) dried pasta
90g (3oz) butter
2 tbsp finely chopped chives
100g (3½oz) salmon caviar
salt, black pepper

Cook pasta in a large pot of boiling, salted water, until firm to the bite. Drain, reserving about ½ cup pasta water. Return pasta with butter and chives to the warm pasta pot. Toss well to coat, adding reserved water as needed. Add caviar and toss carefully to avoid crushing caviar. Add salt and pepper to taste. Serve immediately.

WHICH PASTA?
Thin strands - capellini, spaghettini, paglia e fieno.

COOKS' NOTE
If using capellini or paglia e fieno - called straw and hay - be sure to cook in plenty of boiling water. Stir with a long wooden fork as soon as the pasta is in the water, and drain when pasta is still slightly undercooked.

PRAWNS WITH LEMON AND BASIL

SERVES 4

500g (1lb) dried pasta
350g (12oz) cooked, peeled large prawns
2 garlic cloves, finely chopped
½ red onion, finely chopped
½ tsp crushed chilli flakes
2 tbsp lemon juice
5 tbsp extra virgin olive oil
12 cherry tomatoes, halved
2 tbsp chopped fresh basil
salt, black pepper

Cook pasta in a large pot of boiling, salted water, until firm to the bite if serving hot or just firm to the bite if serving as a salad. While pasta is cooking, combine prawns, garlic, onion, chilli flakes, lemon juice, oil, tomatoes and basil in a bowl. Drain pasta. Return pasta with prawn and tomato mixture to the warm pasta pot. Toss well to coat. Add salt and pepper to taste. Serve immediately or at room temperature.

WHICH PASTA?
Thin strands or medium shells - spaghetti, gnocchi, conchiglie.

THINK AHEAD
Make up to 8 hours in advance if serving as a salad. Cover and refrigerate. Return to room temperature before serving.

COOKS' NOTE
For the most authentic Italian flavour, use a peppery olive oil such as Tuscan or Umbrian.

SCALLOPS WITH GARLIC AND CRISP CRUMBS

SERVES 4

500g (1lb) dried pasta
8 tbsp extra virgin olive oil
2 garlic cloves, finely chopped
2 tbsp chopped fresh flat-leaf parsley
60g (2oz) dried breadcrumbs (see page 160)
½ tsp crushed chilli flakes
12 scallops, cut into quarters, or 24 queen scallops
salt, black pepper

Cook pasta in a large pot of boiling, salted water, until firm to the bite. While pasta is cooking, heat oil in a large frying pan. Add garlic, parsley, breadcrumbs and chilli flakes and cook over a high heat, 1 minute. Add scallops and cook, stirring constantly, until just turning opaque, 1-2 minutes. Add salt and pepper to taste. Drain pasta and add to hot pan. Toss well to coat. Serve immediately.

WHICH PASTA?
Thin to medium ribbons - linguine, fettuccine.

COOKS' NOTE
Timing is everything in this sauce. The pasta must be ready when the scallops are ready. Scallops become tough if overcooked. A sweet olive oil, preferably Ligurian, will best complement the scallops' natural sweetness.

WHITE CLAMS

SERVES 4

1kg (2lb) small clams, in shells	**2 garlic cloves, finely chopped**
125ml (4floz) dry white wine	**2 tbsp finely chopped fresh flat-leaf parsley**
500g (1lb) dried pasta	**additional 2 tbsp extra virgin olive oil**
4 tbsp extra virgin olive oil	
¼ tsp crushed chilli flakes	**salt, black pepper**

Scrub clams under running water. Discard any that are broken or not tightly closed. Place clams with wine in a large pot with a lid on. Steam over medium heat until shells are open, shaking pot occasionally to ensure even cooking, about 4-5 minutes. Use a slotted spoon to lift out clams, and set aside. Discard any that do not open. Tip the pot and slowly pour out the clear clam and wine juices, taking care to leave the sandy residue in the pot. Reserve juices and discard residue. Remove clams from shells and reserve, discarding shells.
Cook pasta in large pot of boiling, salted water, until firm to the bite. While pasta is cooking, heat oil in a large frying pan. Add chilli flakes, garlic and parsley. Cook over medium heat until fragrant, 1 minute. Add reserved clam juices and boil vigorously for 1 minute. Remove from heat.
Drain pasta. Add pasta to hot clam juices. Return to heat and cook, tossing constantly, for 1 minute. Add clams and 2 tbsp olive oil and toss well to coat. Add salt and pepper to taste. Serve immediately.

WHICH PASTA?
Strands or thin ribbons – spaghettini, spaghetti, linguine.

COOKS' NOTE
A simple variation for this recipe is to replace clams with mussels. Cook as directed above. You could leave a handful of mussels in their bottom shells as a garnish.

QUICK COOK
TUNA AND TOMATO

SERVES 4

6 tbsp extra virgin olive oil
1 small onion, finely chopped
2 garlic cloves, crushed
1 - 400g (14oz) tin Italian plum tomatoes, chopped
1 - 200g (7oz) tin tuna in oil, drained and flaked
salt, black pepper
500g (1lb) dried pasta

Heat oil in a large frying pan. Add onion and garlic and cook, stirring constantly over medium high heat, until softened, 5 minutes. Add tomatoes. Simmer rapidly until just thickened, 10 minutes. Add tuna and cook until hot through, 3 minutes. Add salt and pepper to taste. Meanwhile, cook pasta in a large pot of boiling, salted water, until firm to the bite. Drain. Add pasta to the hot sauce. Toss well to coat. Serve immediately.

WHICH PASTA?
Strands, thin ribbons or tubes - spaghetti, linguine or penne.

THINK AHEAD
Make sauce up to 2 days in advance. Cover and refrigerate.

VARIATION
PIQUANT TUNA WITH TOMATOES
Add 1 tbsp rinsed capers and 12 sliced pitted black olives to the pan with the tuna. Finish as directed.

CHILLI SQUID

SERVES 4

500g (1lb) dried pasta
5 tbsp extra virgin olive oil
4 garlic cloves, finely sliced
½ tsp crushed chilli flakes
350g (12oz) squid, cleaned and cut
  into 1cm (½in) rings
2 tbsp lemon juice
2 tbsp finely chopped fresh flat-leaf
  parsley
salt, black pepper

Cook pasta in a large pot of boiling, salted water, until firm to the bite. While pasta is cooking, heat oil in a large frying pan. Add garlic and chilli and cook over high heat until just golden, 1-2 minutes. Add squid and cook, stirring constantly, until opaque, 2-3 minutes. Add lemon juice, parsley and salt and pepper to taste. Drain pasta. Add pasta to the hot squid. Toss well to coat. Serve immediately.

WHICH PASTA?
Strands or thin ribbons - spaghetti, linguine.

COOKS' NOTE
Squid needs to be cooked either quickly over high heat or slowly over low heat to avoid a tough, rubbery texture. In this recipe, be sure to combine with the pasta as soon as the squid is cooked.

VARIATION
CHILLI PRAWNS
Replace squid with 350g (12oz) large raw peeled prawns. Cook as directed until prawns are pink and firm, 3-4 minutes. Finish as directed.

SMOKED SALMON WITH WHITE WINE, CREAM AND CHIVES

SERVES 4

60g (2oz) butter
2 shallots, finely chopped
200ml (7floz) white wine
175ml (6floz) double cream
grated zest of ½ lemon
2 tbsp lemon juice

2 tbsp chopped fresh chives
200g (7oz) smoked salmon slices,
  cut into strips
salt, black pepper
500g (1lb) dried pasta
4 tsp salmon roe, optional

Melt butter in a large frying pan over medium-low heat. Add shallots and cook, stirring occasionally, until soft, 5 minutes. Add wine and simmer until reduced by half, 3 minutes. Add cream, lemon zest and juice, chives and salmon. Heat over medium-low heat, without boiling, until hot through, 1 minute. Add salt and pepper to taste. Meanwhile, cook pasta in a large pot of boiling, salted water, until firm to the bite. Drain, reserving ½ cup pasta water. Add pasta to the hot sauce. Toss well to coat, adding reserved water as needed. Top with salmon roe, if using. Serve immediately.

WHICH PASTA?
Thin to medium ribbons - tagliolini, fettuccine, tagliatelle.

QUICK COOK
SCALLOPS WITH CREME FRAICHE AND DILL

SERVES 4

500g (1lb) dried pasta
60g (2oz) butter
6 spring onions, finely sliced
8 scallops, cut into quarters
3 tbsp crème fraîche
2 tbsp chopped fresh dill
salt, black pepper

Cook pasta in a large pot of boiling, salted water, until firm to the bite. While pasta is cooking, melt butter in a large frying pan over medium heat. Add spring onions and cook, stirring frequently, until soft, 3 minutes. Add scallops and cook, stirring constantly, until just turning opaque, 1-2 minutes. Add crème fraîche and dill. Continue cooking until heated through, 1 minute. Drain pasta, reserving ½ cup pasta water. Add pasta to hot sauce. Toss well to coat, adding reserved water as needed. Add salt and pepper to taste. Serve immediately.

WHICH PASTA?
Thin to medium ribbons - linguine, tagliolini, fettuccine, tagliatelle.

QUICK COOK
SPICY GARLIC PRAWNS WITH CHERRY TOMATOES

SERVES 4

500g (1lb) dried pasta
5 tbsp extra virgin olive oil
½ tsp crushed chilli flakes
4 garlic cloves, finely chopped
500g (1lb) large raw prawns in shells
250g (8oz) cherry tomatoes, halved
salt, black pepper
2 tbsp chopped fresh flat-leaf parsley

Cook pasta in a large pot of boiling, salted water, until just firm to the bite. Heat oil in a large frying pan. Add chilli and garlic and cook over high heat until pale gold, 1 minute. Add prawns and cook, stirring constantly, until just turning pink, 1 minute. Add tomatoes and cook, stirring constantly, until tomatoes are hot and wilted and prawns are firm, 2-3 minutes. Add salt and pepper to taste. Drain pasta. Add drained pasta with parsley to hot sauce. Toss well to coat. Serve immediately.

WHICH PASTA?
Strands and thin ribbons - spaghettini, spaghetti, linguine.

VARIATION
SPICY GARLIC SCALLOPS
Replace prawns with 350g (12oz) scallops, halved. Cook as directed until just opaque, 2-3 minutes. Finish as directed.

SLOW COOK
RED MUSSELS

SERVES 4

FOR TOMATO SAUCE

4 tbsp extra virgin olive oil
2 garlic cloves, finely chopped
¼ tsp crushed chilli flakes
1 - 400g (14oz) tin Italian plum tomatoes, chopped, or
  500g (1lb) fresh ripe tomatoes, peeled and chopped
salt, black pepper

1kg (2lb) mussels
5 tbsp white wine
500g (1lb) dried pasta
2 tbsp fresh flat-leaf parsley, chopped

Heat oil in a large frying pan. Add garlic and chilli and cook
over medium-high heat until just golden, 6 minutes. Add
tomatoes. Simmer rapidly, stirring occasionally, until thick,
15 minutes. Add salt and pepper to taste.
Meanwhile, scrub mussels under running water. Discard any
that are broken or not tightly closed. Place mussels and wine
in a large pot with a lid on. Steam over medium heat, shaking
occasionally, until shells are open, 4-5 minutes. Remove
mussels with a slotted spoon and set aside. Discard any that
do not open. Tip the pot and slowly pour out the clear mussel
juices, taking care to leave the sandy residue in the pot.
Reserve juices and discard residue.
Meanwhile, cook pasta in a large pot of boiling, salted water,
until firm to the bite. Drain pasta and add with mussels,
mussel juices and parsley to the hot sauce. Toss gently.
Serve immediately.

WHICH PASTA?
Strands or thin ribbons - spaghettini, spaghetti, linguine.

THINK AHEAD
Make tomato sauce up to 3 days in advance. Cover and refrigerate. Reheat
before combining with mussels and pasta as directed.

COOKS' NOTE
For a more elegant presentation, remove and discard the empty half of the
mussel shells.

VARIATION
RED CLAMS
Replace mussels with 1kg (2lb) small clams in shells.
Cook as directed.

SLOW COOK
SEAFOOD EXTRAVAGANZA

SERVES 4 - 6

500g (1lb) mussels or small clams in shells
125ml (4floz) white wine
5 tbsp extra virgin olive oil
4 garlic cloves, crushed
8 large raw prawns with shells
4 medium squid, cleaned and cut
  into 1cm (½in) rings
4 cooked langoustines
1 fresh red chilli, finely sliced
4 medium tomatoes, peeled, seeded
  and diced (see pages 156 & 158)
salt, black pepper
500g (1lb) dried pasta
1 handful whole fresh basil leaves
additional extra virgin olive oil for
  drizzling

Scrub mussels or clams under running water. Discard any that are broken or not tightly closed. Place wine and mussels or clams in a large, heavy based pot with a lid over medium-high heat. Cook, shaking pan frequently, until shells open, 4-5 minutes. Remove mussels or clams with a slotted spoon and reserve. Discard any that do not open. Tip pot and slowly pour out clear seafood juices, taking care to leave sandy residue in the pot. Reserve juices and discard residue. Rinse pot.

Heat oil in the pot over high heat. Add garlic and prawns and cook, stirring constantly, until the prawns are just turning pink, 2 minutes. Add the squid, langoustine, chilli and tomatoes. Cook, stirring constantly, until the squid is just opaque, 3-4 minutes. Add reserved seafood juices and heat through, 30 seconds. Add salt and pepper to taste. Remove from heat.

Meanwhile, cook pasta in a large pot of boiling, salted water, until firm to the bite. Drain. Add pasta with basil to the hot sauce. Toss gently to coat. Drizzle over about 1-2 tbsp additional olive oil. Serve immediately.

WHICH PASTA?
Thin strands or ribbons- spaghettini, spaghetti, or linguine.

COOKS' NOTE
For cooking you can use any good extra virgin oil, but for the final drizzle we suggest a peppery extra virgin oil from Puglia or from Tuscany.

Pasta with Meat

MEAT IN THE PASTA PANTRY

Pancetta is an Italian streaky bacon, but it has a distinctly different flavour from regular streaky bacon as it is cured differently. Unsmoked streaky bacon can be used instead, but, for authentic Italian flavour, we urge you to seek out pancetta from Italian speciality or gourmet shops. Buy several pieces about 60g (2oz), each cut into 5-10mm (¼-½ in) slices. Wrap separately and store in the freezer for up to 3 months. This way you will always have the real thing on hand when it is called for.

Prosciutto is a specially cured Italian ham that comes from the hind thigh of the pig and is air-cured for over a year. This long process of air-curing gives it a distinctively sweet flavour and delicate rosy colour. Buy prosciutto sliced to order and avoid the packages of ready sliced meat wherever possible. Store it well wrapped in the refrigerator for no more than three days.

There is an old adage from Parma that says: *Grasso e magro non del tutto, ecco il pregio del prosciutto.* This means that prosciutto must have the right balance of fat and meat. When buying, look for prosciutto with a generous proportion of fat, as this contributes as much to the flavour as the meat part.

The best sausage to use for making pasta sauces is Luganega, a sweet medium-ground sausage. If you cannot find it, use a coarse-ground sausage with a very high percentage of pork meat, such as Cumberland or Toulouse, or any other mild sausage not containing herbs or garlic.

QUICK COOK
PROSCIUTTO AND CREAM

SERVES 4

500g (1lb) dried pasta
60g (2oz) butter
200g (7oz) prosciutto slices, cut
  into strips 1cm (½in) wide
½ small onion, finely chopped
4 tbsp dry white wine
125ml (4floz) double cream
salt, black pepper
4 tbsp freshly grated parmesan,
  plus additional to serve

Cook pasta in a large pot of boiling, salted water, until firm to the bite. While pasta is cooking, melt butter in a large frying pan over medium-low heat. Add prosciutto strips and onion and cook, stirring frequently, until onion is soft, 4-5 minutes. Add wine and raise heat to medium-high. Simmer until just evaporated. Add cream and cook until just thickened, 1 minute. Remove from heat and add salt and pepper to taste. Drain pasta, reserving ½ cup pasta water. Add pasta with parmesan to the hot sauce. Toss well to coat, adding reserved water as needed. Serve immediately with additional parmesan.

WHICH PASTA?
Medium ribbons- fettuccine, tagliatelle.

QUICK COOK
PIZZAIOLA

SERVES 4

2 tbsp extra virgin olive oil
300g (1¾lb) rump steak, cut into strips 5cm (2in) long
  and 1cm (½in) wide
1 - 400g (14oz) tin chopped Italian plum tomatoes
2 garlic cloves, crushed
2 tsp fresh oregano or 1 tsp dried oregano
2 tbsp capers, drained and rinsed
4 tbsp pitted, sliced black olives
500g (1lb) dried pasta
1 tbsp finely chopped fresh flat-leaf parsley

Heat oil in a large frying pan. Add steak and cook over high heat until browned all over, 3 minutes. Remove from pan with slotted spoon, cover to keep warm and reserve. Reduce heat to medium high. Add tomatoes, garlic, oregano, capers and olives. Simmer rapidly, stirring occasionally, until thickened, 10 minutes. Remove pan from heat. Return steak to the pan to keep warm. Meanwhile, cook pasta in a large pot of boiling, salted water. Drain. Add pasta with parsley to the hot sauce. Toss well to coat. Serve immediately.

WHICH PASTA?
Strands - spaghetti, spaghettini.

COOKS' NOTE
This sauce is so called because it contains oregano which, with tomato, is one of the traditional ingredients for pizza.

QUICK COOK
CRISPY PANCETTA AND SPRING ONIONS

SERVES 4

8 pancetta or streaky bacon slices, smoked or
  unsmoked
30g (1oz) butter
2 tbsp extra virgin olive oil
8 spring onions, sliced
500g (1lb) dried pasta
4 tbsp freshly grated parmesan
salt, black pepper
additional freshly grated parmesan to serve

Cook pancetta, turning frequently, in a large frying pan over medium-low heat until browned and crisp, 10 minutes. Drain on paper towels and cut into 2.5cm (1in) wide strips. Pour off excess fat from pan. Add butter and oil to pan and melt over medium heat. Add spring onions and cook, stirring constantly, until just soft, 2 minutes. Meanwhile, cook pasta in a large pot of boiling, salted water, until firm to the bite. Drain, reserving ½ cup pasta water. Add pasta with parmesan and pancetta to spring onions. Toss well to coat, adding reserved water as needed. Add salt and pepper to taste. Serve immediately with additional parmesan.

WHICH PASTA?
Tubes or shapes - penne, rigatoni, gnocchi, conchiglie.

COOKS' NOTE
Try and match the size of the pasta to the size of your ingredients. Cut the pancetta into pieces that can be easily caught in the hollow of the pasta shape.

QUICK COOK
SAUSAGE WITH CREAM AND BASIL

SERVES 4

2 tbsp extra virgin olive oil
1 small onion, finely chopped
4 garlic cloves, crushed
250g (8oz) Italian sausages, skinned
 and crumbled

300ml (10floz) double cream
500g (1lb) dried pasta
1 handful fresh basil leaves, torn
salt, black pepper
freshly grated parmesan to serve

Heat oil in a large frying pan. Add onion and garlic and cook, stirring occasionally over medium-high heat, until just golden, 5 minutes. Add sausage and cook, stirring frequently to break up meat, until it just loses its pink colour, 10 minutes. Stir in cream and simmer until just thickened, 1-2 minutes. Add salt and pepper to taste. Meanwhile, cook pasta in a large pot of boiling, salted water, until firm to the bite. Drain, reserving ½ cup pasta water. Add pasta with basil to the hot sauce. Toss well to coat, adding reserved water as needed. Serve immediately with parmesan.

WHICH PASTA?
Tubes or shapes - conchiglie, fusilli, macaroni.

QUICK COOK
PAN-ROAST CHICKEN WITH GARLIC AND SHALLOTS

SERVES 4-6

4 boneless chicken breasts
12 whole garlic cloves
8 whole shallots
175ml (6floz) white wine
2 tbsp extra virgin olive oil
salt, black pepper
175ml (6floz) double cream
500g (1lb) dried pasta

Preheat oven to 200°C (400°F) Gas 6. Place chicken skin-side up, with garlic and shallots, in a large oven-proof frying pan. Pour over wine. Drizzle chicken skin with oil and sprinkle with salt and pepper. Roast until chicken is cooked through and skin is crisp and golden, 25-30 minutes. Remove chicken, garlic and shallots and cover to keep warm. Bring chicken juices to a simmer over medium high heat. Add cream and cook, stirring constantly, until hot through, 1 minute. Add salt and pepper to taste. Meanwhile, cook pasta in a large pot of boiling, salted water, until firm to the bite. Drain. Add pasta to the hot sauce. Toss well to coat. Slice each chicken breast crosswise into 3 pieces. Top pasta with chicken, garlic and shallots. Serve immediately.

WHICH PASTA?
Medium to wide ribbons or large tubes - tagliatelle, pappardelle, penne, rigatoni.

COOKS' NOTE
Snipping off the tops of the roast garlic and shallots with kitchen scissors makes it easier to squeeze out the soft, sweet cooked centres from their papery skins.

QUICK COOK
AMATRICIANA

SERVES 4

4 tbsp extra virgin olive oil
200g (7oz) unsmoked pancetta or
  streaky bacon, cut into 0.5cm (¼in)
  wide strips
½ tsp crushed chilli flakes
6 tbsp dry white wine
1 onion, finely chopped
1 - 400g (14oz) tin Italian plum
  tomatoes, chopped, or 500g (1lb)
  fresh tomatoes, peeled and chopped
salt, black pepper
500g (1lb) dried pasta
4 tbsp freshly grated pecorino
  romano or parmesan, plus
  additional cheese to serve

Heat oil in a large frying pan. Add
pancetta strips and chilli flakes and cook,
stirring occasionally over medium heat,
until pancetta is crisp, 5 minutes. Add
wine and simmer until reduced by half,
1 minute. Add onion and cook, stirring
frequently, until soft and just golden,
10 minutes. Turn heat to medium-high.
Add tomatoes and cook, until thickened,
10 minutes. Add salt and pepper to taste.
Meanwhile, cook pasta in a large pot of
boiling, salted water, until firm to the
bite. Drain. Add pasta with cheese to
the hot sauce. Toss well to coat. Serve
immediately with additional cheese.

WHICH PASTA?
Strands or tubes - spaghetti, bucatini, penne,
rigatoni.

THINK AHEAD
Make sauce up to 1 day in advance. Cool
completely. Cover and refrigerate.

COOKS' NOTE
This sauce is made in the Apennines east of Rome
for the local Festa on 15th August. The cheese
used in the traditional recipe is Pecorino, which
has the right piquancy to match the flavour of the
chilli. If you cannot find Pecorino Romano, you can
use Parmesan. The pancetta should be unsmoked.

QUICK COOK
CHICKEN WITH LEMON AND MUSHROOMS

SERVES 4

30g (1oz) butter
2 skinless, boneless chicken breasts, cut across into
  8 - 2.5 cm (1in) wide strips
2 garlic cloves, crushed
250g (8oz) brown mushrooms, sliced
1 tsp fresh thyme leaves
2 tbsp lemon juice
salt, black pepper
500g (1lb) dried pasta
additional 30g (1oz) butter to toss

Melt butter in a large frying pan over medium heat. Add chicken strips and cook,
stirring frequently, until opaque, 4 minutes. Add garlic, mushrooms and thyme.
Cook, stirring frequently, until mushrooms are soft and chicken is cooked through,
4 minutes. Add lemon juice and salt and pepper to taste. Meanwhile, cook pasta in
a large pot of boiling, salted water, until firm to the bite. Drain. Add pasta to hot
sauce with additional butter. Toss well to coat. Serve immediately.

WHICH PASTA?
Medium to large ribbons - fettuccine, tagliatelle, pappardelle.

THINK AHEAD
Make sauce up to 1 day in advance. Cover and refrigerate. Reheat gently, adding 2 tbsp water.

QUICK COOK
VENETIAN-STYLE CHICKEN LIVER

SERVES 4

250g (8oz) chicken livers
30g (1oz) butter
3 tbsp extra virgin olive oil
1 garlic clove, lightly crushed
4 fresh sage leaves
4 tbsp dry white wine
salt, black pepper
500g (1lb) dried pasta
4 tbsp freshly grated parmesan
15g (½oz) additional butter to toss
freshly grated parmesan to serve

Place chicken livers in sieve and rinse under cold running water. Drain and pat dry with kitchen paper. Cut each chicken liver into 3 pieces, discarding membranes and gristle. Melt butter with olive oil in a large frying pan over medium heat. Add garlic and sage and cook until garlic is golden, 2-3 minutes. Remove and discard garlic and sage. Add chicken livers and cook, stirring frequently, until browned, 1 minute. Add wine and simmer until just evaporated, 30 seconds. Add salt and pepper to taste. Meanwhile, cook pasta in a large pot of boiling, salted water, until firm to the bite. Drain. Add pasta with parmesan and additional butter to the hot sauce. Toss well to coat. Serve immediately with parmesan.

WHICH PASTA?
Shapes or medium to wide ribbons - conchiglie, farfalle, tagliatelle, pappardelle.

COOKS' NOTE
Quick cooking ensures that the chicken liver pieces will be still pink and juicy inside.

QUICK COOK
CARBONARA

SERVES 4

3 egg yolks
8 tbsp freshly grated parmesan
2 tbsp oil
2 garlic cloves, peeled and halved
200g (7oz) unsmoked pancetta or
  unsmoked streaky bacon slices,
  cut into 0.5cm (¼in) wide strips
4 tbsp white wine
500g (1lb) dried pasta
15g (½oz) butter
salt, black pepper
additional freshly grated parmesan
  to serve

Mix egg yolks and parmesan in a bowl until combined. Heat oil in a large frying pan. Add garlic and cook over medium-high heat until golden, 2 minutes. Remove garlic and discard. Add pancetta and cook, stirring occasionally, until crisp, 5 minutes. Add wine and simmer until just evaporated, 2 minutes. Remove from heat.
Meanwhile, cook pasta in a large pot of boiling, salted water, until firm to the bite. Drain, reserving ½ cup pasta water. Add drained pasta to the hot pancetta and toss well to coat. Remove from the heat. Add egg mixture and butter and toss again to coat, adding reserved water as needed. Add salt and pepper to taste. Serve immediately with additional parmesan.

WHICH PASTA?
Hollow or thin strands - bucatini, spaghetti.

COOKS' NOTE
We have sharpened the sauce with the addition of white wine. If you don't have any white wine in the pantry, use 2 tbsp dry vermouth instead.

SLOW COOK
SPICY SAUSAGE RAGU

SERVES 4

3 tbsp extra virgin olive oil
1 onion, finely chopped
2 garlic cloves, finely chopped
250g (8oz) Italian sausages, skinned and crumbled
¾ tsp crushed chilli flakes
1 tsp fennel seeds
1 tsp dried oregano
1 tbsp tomato purée
1 – 400g (14oz) tin chopped Italian plum tomatoes
150ml (5floz) double cream
salt, black pepper
500g (1lb) dried pasta
freshly grated parmesan to serve

Heat oil in a large frying pan. Cook onion and garlic over medium-high heat, stirring frequently, until soft and pale gold, 5 minutes. Add sausage. Cook, stirring to break up, until coloured, 10 minutes. Add chilli flakes, fennel, oregano, tomato purée and chopped tomatoes. Simmer, stirring occasionally, until thickened, 20 minutes. Add cream. Cook, stirring until heated through. Add salt and pepper to taste.

Meanwhile, cook pasta in a large pot of boiling, salted water, until firm to the bite. Drain. Add pasta to the hot sauce. Toss well to coat. Serve immediately with parmesan.

WHICH PASTA?
Medium or large tubes - ditali, penne, rigatoni, macaroni.

THINK AHEAD
Make ragù up to 3 days in advance. Cover and refrigerate. Alternatively, freeze up to 1 month in advance. Defrost overnight in refrigerator before reheating.

COOK'S NOTE
If you can't find Italian sausages, use the best, coarse-ground sausage you can buy. A good quality Cumberland or Toulouse sausage is a reasonable substitute.

SLOW COOK
CLASSIC RAGU BOLOGNESE

SERVES 4 - 6

60g (2oz) butter
2 tbsp extra virgin olive oil
60g (2oz) unsmoked pancetta or unsmoked streaky bacon, finely chopped
1 small onion, finely chopped
1 carrot, finely chopped
1 celery stalk, finely chopped
1 garlic clove, finely chopped
1 bay leaf
500g (1lb) lean chuck steak, coarsely minced
2 tbsp tomato purée
150ml (5floz) red wine
150ml (5floz) meat stock, or water
150ml (5floz) milk
salt, black pepper, nutmeg
500g (1lb) dried pasta
freshly grated parmesan to serve

Melt butter and oil in a large, heavy-based pot over medium-high heat. Add pancetta and cook, stirring frequently, until coloured, 5 minutes. Add onion, carrot, celery, garlic and bay leaf and cook, stirring frequently, until soft, 8 minutes. Add minced steak and cook, crumbling with a fork to break up, until browned. Turn heat to medium. Add tomato purée and cook, stirring constantly, 1 minute. Add wine and stock or water. Bring to a boil, then turn heat down to very low. Simmer, partially covered, stirring occasionally and adding milk 2 tbsp at a time every 20-30 minutes. Cook until thick and rich, 2 hours. Add salt, pepper and nutmeg to taste.

Meanwhile, cook pasta in a large pot of boiling, salted water until firm to the bite. Drain. Add drained pasta to hot ragù. Toss well to coat. Serve immediately with parmesan.

WHICH PASTA?
Medium ribbons or large tubes - tagliatelle, macaroni, rigatoni, penne.

THINK AHEAD
Make sauce up to 3 days in advance. Cover and refrigerate. Alternatively, make up to 1 month in advance and freeze. Defrost overnight in refrigerator before reheating.

SLOW COOK
RAGU AL FORNO

SERVES 4 - 6

500g (1lb) dried pasta
1 recipe classic ragù bolognese (see page 91)
3 tbsp freshly grated parmesan

FOR BECHAMEL
60g (2oz) butter
3 tbsp flour
500ml (16floz) milk
salt, pepper, nutmeg

Preheat oven to 200°C (400°F) Gas 6.

For bechamel, melt butter over medium heat in a heavy saucepan. Whisk in flour and cook until foaming, about 1 minute. Remove from heat and pour in milk gradually, whisking constantly. Return to heat and cook, whisking constantly, until sauce thickens, about 2 minutes. Bring to the boil and remove from heat. Add salt, black pepper and nutmeg to taste. Meanwhile, cook pasta in a large pot of boiling, salted water, until just firm to the bite. Drain. Toss pasta with ragù, bechamel and parmesan. Place in buttered 30cm x 20cm x 7.5cm (12in x 8in x 3in) oven-proof dish and bake until golden and crusty, 15 minutes. Leave to stand for 5 minutes before serving.

WHICH PASTA?
Large tubes or shells - rigatoni, penne, conchiglie.

THINK AHEAD
Assemble and leave cool completely. Cover, unbaked and refrigerate up to 1 day in advance. Alternatively, freeze up to 3 weeks in advance. Defrost overnight in the refrigerator.

SLOW COOK
CHICKEN, TOMATO AND ROSEMARY RAGU

SERVES 4

FOR CHICKEN
350g (12oz) boneless, skinless chicken thighs
1 celery stalk, quartered
½ small onion, chopped
5 tbsp dry white wine

FOR SAUCE
5 tbsp extra virgin olive oil
1 tbsp finely chopped onion
1 tbsp finely chopped celery stalk
3 garlic cloves, finely chopped
1 tbsp finely chopped fresh flat-leaf parsley
1 tbsp finely chopped rosemary
grated zest of ½ lemon
1 - 400g (14oz) tin Italian plum tomatoes, chopped
salt, black pepper
500g (1lb) dried pasta

Place chicken, celery, onion and wine in a pan with cold water to cover. Bring slowly to a simmer over medium-low heat. Simmer gently without boiling until cooked through, 7-10 minutes. Cool completely in cooking liquid. Drain, reserving liquid, and cut chicken into 1cm (½in) dice.

Heat oil in a large frying pan. Add onion and celery and cook, stirring occasionally, over medium-low heat until soft, 5 minutes. Add garlic, parsley and rosemary and cook until fragrant, 1 minute. Add lemon zest, tomatoes and 4 tbsp reserved poaching liquid. Reduce heat to low and simmer gently, stirring occasionally, until thick, 30 minutes. Add salt and pepper to taste. Add chicken and heat through, 5 minutes. Meanwhile, cook pasta in a large pot of boiling, salted water, until firm to the bite. Drain. Add pasta to the hot sauce. Toss well to coat. Serve immediately.

WHICH PASTA?
Medium tubes or shells - conchiglie, gnocchetti, macaroni.

THINK AHEAD
Cook chicken, but do not dice, up to 2 days in advance. Make tomato sauce up to 1 day in advance. Cover and refrigerate.

SLOW COOK
CLASSIC LASAGNE AL FORNO

SERVES 4

12 sheets dried or fresh lasagne
1 recipe classic ragù bolognese (see page 91)
6 tbsp freshly grated parmesan

FOR BECHAMEL

75g (2½oz) butter
4½ tbsp flour
750ml (1¼ pints) milk
salt, black pepper, nutmeg

Preheat oven to 200°C (400°F) Gas 6.
Cook pasta, 3 sheets at a time, in a large pot of boiling, salted water for half the recommended time, or until pasta is pliable but slightly hard at the centre, about 4 minutes for dried pasta, 1 minute for fresh pasta. Drain and place sheets in a single layer on tea towels.
For bechamel, melt butter over medium heat in a heavy saucepan. Whisk in flour and cook until foaming, about 1 minute. Remove from heat and pour in milk gradually, whisking constantly. Return to heat and cook, whisking constantly, until sauce thickens, about 2 minutes. Bring to the boil and remove from the heat. Add salt, pepper and nutmeg to taste.
In a buttered 30cm x 20cm x 7.5cm (12in x 8in x 3in) oven-proof dish, spread a thin layer of the bechamel. Lay 3 sheets pasta, over the bechamel. Spread a quarter of the ragù over the pasta. Spread a quarter of the bechamel over the ragù, and sprinkle with a quarter of the parmesan. Starting with another layer of 3 pasta sheets, repeat layers. Repeat layers again to finish, ending with parmesan. Bake in oven until golden and bubbling, 30 minutes. Leave to stand for 5 minutes before serving.

WHICH PASTA?
Egg lasagne, green or yellow, fresh when possible.

THINK AHEAD
Assemble lasagne and leave to cool completely. Cover, unbaked, and refrigerate up to 1 day in advance. Alternatively freeze, unbaked, up to 3 weeks in advance. Defrost overnight in refrigerator. Cook in preheated 200°C (400°F) Gas 6 oven for 30 minutes.
Make bechamel up to 2 days in advance. Cover with clingfilm, pressing down on the surface to prevent a skin forming. Refrigerate. Before using, beat to make it easy to spread. If making with cold bechamel, be sure to have ragù and pasta also cold.

COOKS' NOTE
We don't recommend no-cook lasagne, but if it is all you can find on the supermarket shelves, always treat it as regular dried lasagne and pre-cook until just pliable, about 30 seconds. Alternatively, follow the lasagne recipe on the packet, which will make proper allowances for the amount of liquid absorbed by the lasagne during baking.

VARIATION
CLASSIC ITALIAN-AMERICAN LASAGNE
Omit bechamel. Use 250g (8oz) ricotta, crumbled, and 250g (8oz) finely sliced mozzarella in place of bechamel. Arrange in layers as directed, substituting ricotta and mozzarella mixture for bechamel. Bake as directed.

Puglie

A deliciously fruity filtered
Ogliarola and Barese olives

EXCLUSIVELY IMF

Pasta with Olives and Olive Oil

OLIVE OIL IN THE PASTA PANTRY

Always use olive oil when cooking pasta sauces.

We buy extra virgin olive oil, which is made from the first pressing of the olives. It may cost a little more, but its superior quality makes it worth the extra expense. The relative cost of good extra virgin olive oil is not excessive when compared to a bottle of fine wine, which is finished at one sitting.

However, there is no need to use the best quality olive oil for everything. It is a good idea to have at least 2 bottles on the go at once. You can use a lighter, less costly oil for cooking and keep a superior one for seasoning and drizzling. Although both oils should be extra virgin, there's no need to buy anything but the least expensive available to use for cooking. Your choice of oil for drizzling and tossing is entirely personal. It shouldn't necessarily be Italian; we suggest that you try out a few, from different regions in Italy as well as from different countries, until you find one you like.

The colour of olive oil is dependent upon the timing of the harvest – the very dark green olive oil is from an early harvest, while later harvests yield golden oil – but this is not in itself an indication of quality. Unlike wine, olive oil does not improve with age. It is best stored in a cool, dark place at around 10°C-15°C (50°F-60°F) and should not be kept for longer than 1 year, as, after a year, many oils will start to taste stale.

Green and black olives are not interchangeable. Their taste and texture are different. Black olives owe their dark, rich flavour to being harvested when fully ripe. Green olives are picked before they are ripe and have a firm texture and a tangy taste. Olives are best bought loose and in small quantities as they will spoil within a few days unless generously covered with olive oil. Always have a few jars or tins of good quality olives on hand as a standby.

NO COOK
OLIVE OIL

SERVES 4

**500g (1lb) dried pasta
8 tbsp extra virgin olive oil
salt, crushed chilli flakes**

Cook pasta in a large pot of boiling, salted water, until firm to the bite. Drain, reserving ½ cup pasta water. Toss pasta with oil, adding reserved water as needed. Add salt and chilli flakes to taste.

WHICH PASTA?
Strands - spaghettini, spaghetti.

COOKS' NOTE
We like to use a rich, peppery Tuscan or Umbrian olive oil for this recipe, where the flavour of the olive oil is so important.

VARIATIONS
LEMON OLIVE OIL
Add ½ tsp grated lemon zest and 2 tbsp lemon juice with the olive oil to pasta.

GARLIC OLIVE OIL
Add 2 crushed garlic cloves with the olive oil to pasta.

FRESH HERB OLIVE OIL
Add 1 handful of fresh flat-leaf parsley or basil, chopped, with the olive oil to pasta.

NO COOK
CHILLI OLIVE PESTO

SERVES 4

**125g (4oz) pitted black or
  green olives
1 garlic clove, crushed
½ tsp crushed chilli flakes
6 tbsp extra virgin olive oil
500g (1lb) dried pasta
salt, black pepper**

Place olives, garlic, chilli flakes and oil
in a food processor or blender; pulse
until blended but still retaining some
texture. Cook pasta in a large pot of
boiling, salted water, until firm to the
bite if serving hot or just firm to the bite
if serving as a salad. Drain, reserving
½ cup pasta water. Return pasta with
pesto to the warm pasta pot. Toss well
to coat, adding reserved water as needed.
Add salt and pepper to taste. Serve
immediately or at room temperature.

WHICH PASTA?
Strands or thin ribbons - spaghetti, spaghettini,
linguine.

NO COOK
OLIVE, ANCHOVY AND
CAPER PESTO

SERVES 4

**125g (4oz) pitted black olives
4 anchovy fillets, drained
2 tbsp drained capers, rinsed
1 garlic clove, crushed
¼ tsp dried thyme
6 tbsp olive oil
500g (1lb) dried pasta**

Place olives, anchovies, capers, garlic,
thyme and oil in a food processor or
blender; pulse to a paste. Cook pasta in a
large pot of boiling, salted water, until
firm to the bite if serving hot or just firm
to the bite if serving as a salad. Drain,
reserving ½ cup pasta water. Return
pasta with pesto to the warm pasta
pot. Toss well to coat, adding reserved
water as needed. Serve immediately or
at room temperature.

WHICH PASTA?
Small shapes - pennette, conchiglie, fusilli.

THINK AHEAD
Make pestos up to 4 days in advance. Cover and
refrigerate. If serving as a salad, dress pasta up
to 8 hours in advance. Cover and store at room
temperature.

QUICK COOK
SPICY LEMON OLIVE

SERVES 4

500g (1lb) dried pasta
5 tbsp extra virgin olive oil
2 wide strips thinly pared lemon rind
1 - 50g (1¾oz) tin anchovy fillets,
  drained and chopped
15 pitted black olives, sliced
2 cloves garlic, finely chopped
½ tsp crushed chilli flakes
salt, black pepper
4 tbsp chopped fresh flat-leaf parsley
freshly grated pecorino romano
  to serve

Cook pasta in a large pot of boiling,
salted water, until firm to the bite. While
pasta is cooking, heat oil in a large frying
pan. Add lemon rind and cook over low
heat until sizzling, 2 minutes. Add
anchovies and cook, stirring constantly,
until disintegrated, 2-3 minutes. Add
olives, garlic and chilli flakes. Cook
until fragrant, 2 minutes. Add salt and
pepper to taste. Remove and discard
lemon rind. Drain pasta, reserving ½ cup
pasta water. Add pasta with parsley to
the hot sauce. Toss well to coat, adding
reserved water as needed. Serve
immediately with pecorino.

WHICH PASTA?
Shapes or shells - fusilli, conchiglie, farfalle.

COOKS' NOTE
Preserved anchovy fillets must be cooked over
a gentle heat or they will become bitter. We
recommend either Tuscan or Pugliese olive oil
in this recipe.

PASTA WITH GREENS AND HERBS

GREENS AND HERBS IN THE PASTA PANTRY

When buying fresh herbs, choose as you would fresh flowers. They should be vibrant green and bursting with life. The less fresh the herb, the less flavour it has. Fresh parsley and basil are the most essential fresh herbs in the pasta pantry, and dried just will not do as an alternative.

We prefer flat-leaf parsley, as it is more aromatic than the curly variety. Chopped parsley freezes well; store in an airtight container and scoop out a tablespoon or so as needed. Basil is best torn rather than chopped, as chopping damages its delicate flavour and colour.

Bunches of fresh herbs can be stored in the refrigerator, either in a glass of water with a plastic bag placed loosely over them, or in a plastic tub with their stalks removed. Choose greens that are firm, crisp and fresh looking. Cauliflower and broccoli should have juicy-looking stalks that show no signs of discolouring. Choose bright-looking courgettes that are very firm. When buying fresh peas, look for bright, snappy pods. Frozen peas are a perfectly acceptable substitute for fresh; in fact they are highly preferable to anything but locally grown new season peas in the pod.

NO COOK
SIMPLE BASIL PESTO

SERVES 4

60g (2oz) fresh basil leaves
2 garlic cloves
2 tbsp pine nuts
100ml (3½ floz) extra virgin olive oil
7 tbsp freshly grated parmesan
salt

500g (1lb) dried pasta

Place basil, garlic, pine nuts and olive oil in a food processor; pulse until smooth. Transfer to a bowl. Stir in parmesan until well combined. Add salt to taste. Set aside or store, see below. Cook pasta in a large pot of boiling, salted water, until firm to the bite if serving hot or just firm to the bite if serving as a salad. Drain pasta, reserving ½ cup pasta water. Return pasta with the pesto to the warm pasta pot. Toss well to coat, adding reserved water as needed. Serve immediately or at room temperature.

WHICH PASTA?
Thin ribbons or strands - trenette, linguine, spaghetti, spaghettini.

THINK AHEAD
Make pesto up to 4 days in advance. Cover and refrigerate. Alternatively, make pesto without parmesan and freeze for up to 3 months. Add parmesan and seasoning when defrosted. If serving as a salad, dress pasta up to 8 hours in advance. Cover and store at room temperature.

COOKS' NOTE
Traditionally, pesto is made only with a sweet-flavoured olive oil, such as Ligurian.

VARIATIONS
BEST BASIL PESTO
Make pesto as directed, adding 3 tbsp softened unsalted butter to the basil mixture with the parmesan.

BASIL PESTO CREAM
Make pesto as directed, adding 3 tbsp Greek-style yoghurt or crème fraîche to the basil mixture with the parmesan.

NO COOK
EVEN SIMPLER BASIL PESTO

SERVES 4

500g (1lb) dried pasta
60g (2oz) fresh basil leaves, torn
2 tbsp pine nuts, toasted (see page 160)
2 garlic cloves, crushed
6 tbsp freshly grated parmesan
7 tbsp extra virgin olive oil
salt

Cook pasta in a large pot of boiling, salted water, until just firm to taste. Drain, reserving ½ cup pasta water. Return pasta with basil, pine nuts, garlic, parmesan and oil to the warm pasta pot. Toss well to coat, adding reserved water as needed. Add salt to taste. Serve immediately.

WHICH PASTA?
Shapes or tubes - conchiglie, penne, ditali.

NO COOK
SPINACH AND WALNUT PESTO

SERVES 4

45g (1½oz) stemmed spinach leaves
4 garlic cloves, crushed
3 tbsp walnut pieces
6 tbsp extra virgin olive oil
8 tbsp freshly grated parmesan
salt, black pepper
500g (1lb) dried pasta

Place spinach, garlic, walnuts and oil in a food processor
or blender; pulse until smooth. Transfer to a bowl. Mix in
parmesan until well combined. Add salt and pepper to taste.
Set aside or store, see below.
Cook pasta in a large pot of boiling, salted water until firm
to the bite if serving hot or just firm to the bite if serving as a
salad. Drain, reserving ½ cup pasta water. Return pasta with
pesto to the warm pasta pot. Toss well to coat, adding reserved
water as needed. Serve immediately or at room temperature.

WHICH PASTA?
Large pasta tubes or shells - rigatoni, gnocchetti rigati, conchiglie.

THINK AHEAD
Make pesto up to 4 days in advance. Cover and refrigerate. Alternatively, make
pesto without cheese and freeze for up to 3 months. Add cheese and seasoning
when defrosted. If serving as a salad, dress pasta up to 8 hours in advance. Cover
and store at room temperature.

VARIATION
PARSLEY PESTO
Replace spinach with 45g (1½oz) fresh flat-leaf parsley. Make
as directed.

QUICK COOK
FRAGRANT FRESH HERB

SERVES 4

500g (1lb) dried pasta
8 tbsp extra virgin olive oil
**1 garlic clove, finely
chopped**
**1 handful fresh flat-leaf
parsley, finely chopped**

**2 tbsp finely chopped
fresh oregano, marjoram
or basil**
**½ tbsp finely chopped fresh
rosemary, thyme or sage**
salt, black pepper

Cook pasta in a large pot of boiling, salted water, until firm to
the bite. While pasta is cooking, heat oil in a large frying pan.
Add garlic and herbs, and cook over medium heat until fragrant,
1 minute. Add salt and pepper to taste. Drain pasta, reserving
½ cup pasta water. Add pasta to the hot sauce. Toss well to
coat, adding reserved water as needed. Serve immediately.

WHICH PASTA?
Thin ribbons - linguine, spaghettini.

COOKS' NOTE
You can vary the kind of herbs, depending on what you have in the garden or
you find in the shop, but parsley must always be included.

QUICK COOK
SIZZLING SAGE BUTTER

SERVES 4

500g (1lb) dried pasta
90g (3oz) butter
2 garlic cloves, peeled and halved
16 fresh sage leaves
freshly grated parmesan to serve

Cook pasta in a large pot of boiling, salted water, until firm to the bite. While pasta is cooking, heat butter and garlic in a small frying pan over a medium heat until just golden. Add sage leaves and cook, stirring, until fragrant, 30 seconds. Remove and discard garlic. Drain pasta and return to the warm pasta pot. Add hot butter and sage to pasta. Toss well to coat. Serve immediately with plenty of parmesan.

WHICH PASTA?
Medium ribbons or stuffed pasta - fettuccine, tagliatelle, ravioli, tortellini, cappelletti.

QUICK COOK
FRESH HERBS AND GOLDEN CRUMBS

SERVES 4

500g (1lb) dried pasta
5 tbsp extra virgin olive oil
75g (2½oz) fresh breadcrumbs
4 spring onions, finely chopped
1 handful fresh flat-leaf parsley, basil, oregano or a combination
additional olive oil
salt, black pepper

Cook pasta in a large pot of boiling, salted water, until firm to the bite. While pasta is cooking, heat oil in a large frying pan. Add breadcrumbs and cook, stirring constantly over medium-high heat, until crisp and golden, 5-8 minutes. Add spring onions and your choice of herbs and stir to combine. Drain pasta. Add drained pasta to the crumbs with 2 tbsp additional oil. Toss to coat. Add salt and pepper to taste. Serve immediately.

WHICH PASTA?
Strands or shapes - spaghetti, conchiglie, fusilli.

QUICK COOK
COURGETTE AND BASIL WITH CREAM

SERVES 4

30g (1oz) butter
2 tbsp extra virgin olive oil
500g (1lb) small courgettes, cut
  into 0.5cm (¼in) thick slices
4 garlic cloves, finely chopped
300ml (10floz) double cream
1 handful torn fresh basil leaves
salt, black pepper
500g (1lb) dried pasta
4 tbsp freshly grated parmesan,
  plus additional to serve

Melt butter with olive oil in a large frying pan. Add courgettes and cook, stirring frequently over medium-high heat, until just golden, 10 minutes. Reduce heat to medium-low. Add garlic and cook, stirring occasionally, until courgettes are soft, 5-10 minutes. Add cream and simmer gently until just thickened, 2 minutes. Add basil with salt and pepper to taste. Meanwhile, cook pasta in a large pot of boiling, salted water, until firm to the bite. Drain. Add pasta with parmesan to the hot sauce. Toss well to coat. Serve immediately with additional parmesan.

WHICH PASTA?
Tubes or shapes - farfalle, penne, ditali.

VARIATION
COURGETTE WITH HAM
Add 4 ham slices cut into short, fine strips, 2.5cm (1in) long and 0.5cm (¼in) wide, to the courgettes with the garlic. Finish as directed.

QUICK COOK
PEAS, PROSCIUTTO AND FRESH HERBS

SERVES 4

500g (1lb) fresh peas (unshelled weight) or
  250g (8oz) tiny frozen peas, defrosted
500g (1lb) dried pasta
90g (3oz) butter
125g (4oz) prosciutto slices, cut into short, fine strips,
  about 2.5cm (1in) long and 0.5cm (¼in) wide
salt, black pepper
6 tbsp freshly grated parmesan
2 tbsp finely chopped fresh mint, basil or flat-leaf parsley, optional
additional freshly grated parmesan to serve

If using fresh peas, cook in boiling, salted water until just tender, 5-8 minutes. Drain. Cook pasta in a large pot of boiling, salted water, until firm to the bite. While pasta is cooking, melt butter in a large frying pan. Add peas and prosciutto and cook, stirring constantly over medium heat, until hot through, 2 minutes. Add salt and pepper to taste. Drain pasta, reserving ½ cup pasta water. Add pasta with parmesan and your chosen herb, if using, to the hot sauce. Toss well to coat, adding reserved water as needed. Serve immediately with additional parmesan.

WHICH PASTA?
Medium to wide ribbons - fettuccine, tagliatelle, pappardelle.

VARIATION
ASPARAGUS, PROSCIUTTO AND FRESH HERBS
Omit peas. Cook 250g (8oz) small asparagus tips in boiling salted water until just tender, 2-3 minutes. Finish as directed.

QUICK COOK
SPICY BROCCOLI WITH GOLDEN GARLIC

SERVES 4

**500g (1lb) broccoli, stalks chopped
and head separated into florets
7 tbsp extra virgin olive oil
4 garlic cloves, finely sliced
½ tsp crushed chilli flakes
salt, black pepper
500g (1lb) dried pasta**

Cook broccoli in a pan of boiling, salted water until just tender, 3-5 minutes. Heat oil in a large frying pan. Add garlic and cook over medium-high heat until just golden, 2 minutes. Add drained broccoli and chilli flakes and cook, stirring occasionally, for 5 minutes. Add salt and pepper to taste. Meanwhile, cook pasta in a large pot of boiling, salted water until firm to the bite. Drain. Add pasta to the hot sauce. Toss well to coat. Serve immediately.

WHICH PASTA?
Shapes - orecchiette, gnocchi, conchiglie.

COOKS' NOTE
We like to use a peppery olive oil from Puglia or Tuscany in this recipe to complement the spicy chilli flakes.

VARIATIONS
SPICY BROCCOLI WITH GOLDEN GARLIC AND ANCHOVIES
Add 4 drained, chopped anchovies to the oil with the garlic. Finish as directed.

SPICY CAULIFLOWER WITH GOLDEN GARLIC
Omit broccoli. Cook 500g (1lb) cauliflower florets in boiling, salted water until just tender, 5-7 minutes. Drain. Finish sauce as directed.

SPICY SPROUTING BROCCOLI WITH GOLDEN GARLIC
Omit broccoli. Replace with 500g (1lb) coarsely chopped sprouting broccoli. Finish as directed.

QUICK COOK
ASPARAGUS WITH CREAM

SERVES 4

**500g (1lb) asparagus, cut into 2.5cm (1in) pieces,
using only tips and tender parts of stem
500g (1lb) dried pasta
75g (2½oz) unsalted butter
2 tbsp finely chopped onion
150ml (5floz) double cream
nutmeg, salt, black pepper
2 tbsp freshly grated parmesan, plus additional to serve**

Cook asparagus in a pan of boiling, salted water until just tender, 3-5 minutes. Drain and plunge into cold water to cool completely. Drain and reserve. Cook pasta in a large pot of boiling, salted water, until firm to the bite. While pasta is cooking, melt butter in a large frying pan. Add onion and cook, stirring occasionally over medium heat, until soft, 5 minutes. Add asparagus and cream and simmer gently until the cream is just thickened, 1-2 minutes. Add nutmeg, salt and pepper to taste. Drain pasta, reserving ½ cup pasta water. Add drained pasta with parmesan to the hot sauce. Toss gently, being careful not to break up asparagus tips and adding reserved water as needed. Serve immediately with additional parmesan.

WHICH PASTA?
Medium tubes or ribbons - ditali, macaroni, fettuccine, tagliatelle.

QUICK COOK
SHREDDED COURGETTES WITH GOLDEN GARLIC

SERVES 4

500g (1lb) dried pasta
6 tbsp extra virgin olive oil
4-6 garlic cloves, finely sliced
4 medium courgettes, grated
salt, black pepper
8 tbsp freshly grated parmesan, plus additional to serve

Cook pasta in a large pot of boiling, salted water, until firm to the bite. While pasta is cooking, heat oil in a large frying pan. Add garlic and cook over high heat until just golden, 2 minutes. Add courgettes and cook, stirring constantly, until soft, 5 minutes. Add salt and pepper to taste. Drain pasta, reserving ½ cup pasta water. Add drained pasta with parmesan to the hot courgettes. Toss well to coat, adding reserved water as needed. Serve immediately with additional parmesan.

WHICH PASTA?

Medium shapes or ribbons - gnocchi, conchiglie, orecchiette, linguine, fettuccine, tagliatelle.

VARIATIONS

WILTED SPINACH WITH GOLDEN GARLIC

Omit courgettes. Use 500g (1lb) spinach, stemmed and roughly chopped. Cook garlic as directed. Add spinach and cook, stirring constantly, until soft, 2 minutes. Finish as directed.

WILTED LEEKS WITH GOLDEN GARLIC

Omit courgettes. Use 3 medium leeks, halved lengthwise and finely sliced. Cook garlic as directed. Add leeks and cook, stirring constantly, until wilted, 5 minutes. Cover and cook, stirring occasionally, until soft, 10 minutes. Finish as directed.

PRIMAVERA

SERVES 4

60g (2oz) butter
2 tbsp extra virgin olive oil
1 tbsp finely chopped onion
1 small garlic clove, finely chopped
1 medium carrot, diced
1 medium celery stalk, diced
1 small courgette, diced
125g (4oz) green beans, cut into 1cm (½in) pieces
**125g (4oz) asparagus, tips cut into 2.5cm (1in) lengths
  and tender parts of stem cut into 1cm (½in) pieces**
**125g (4oz) tiny frozen peas, defrosted, or 250g (8oz)
  (unshelled weight) fresh peas, shelled**
175ml - 250ml (6floz - 8floz) chicken or vegetable stock
salt, black pepper
freshly grated parmesan to serve

Melt butter with oil in a large frying pan over medium low heat. Add onion and cook, stirring constantly, until just soft, 3 minutes. Add garlic, carrot, celery, courgette, green beans, asparagus and peas and cook, stirring frequently, until almost tender, 10 minutes. Add stock just to cover and simmer gently until the liquid has almost evaporated and the vegetables are soft, 10 minutes. Add salt and pepper to taste. Meanwhile, cook pasta in a large pot of boiling, salted water, until firm to the bite. Drain. Add drained pasta to the hot sauce. Toss well to coat. Serve immediately with parmesan.

WHICH PASTA?
Strands, thin ribbons or shapes - spaghetti, linguine, farfalle, gnocchi, conchiglie.

THINK AHEAD
Make sauce up to 1 day in advance. Cool completely. Cover and refrigerate. Reheat slowly over low heat, stirring gently.

VARIATIONS
PRIMAVERA WITH CREAM
Make sauce as directed using only 45g (1½oz) butter. Stir in 150ml (5floz) double cream to finished sauce. Simmer gently until just thickened, 2 minutes. Serve as directed.

PRIMAVERA PESTO
Make sauce as directed. Add 4 tbsp simple basil pesto (see page 105) or storebought basil pesto, with the drained pasta, to the hot sauce. Serve as directed.

SLOW COOK
SPINACH AND RICOTTA LASAGNE

SERVES 4

12 sheets dried or fresh egg lasagne
1kg (2lb) spinach, washed
250g (8oz) ricotta, crumbled
30g (1oz) butter, melted
salt, black pepper, nutmeg
8 tbsp freshly grated parmesan

FOR BECHAMEL
75g (2½oz) butter
4½ tbsp plain flour
750ml (1¼ pints) milk
salt, black pepper, nutmeg

Preheat oven to 180°C (350°F) Gas 4.

Cook pasta, 3 sheets at a time, in a large pot of boiling, salted water for half the time recommended on the package, or until pasta is pliable but slightly hard at the centre, 4 minutes for dried pasta, 1 minute for fresh pasta. Drain and place sheets in a single layer on tea towels.

Place wet spinach in a dry pan. Cover pan and place over medium heat and cook until tender, stirring frequently, about 5 minutes. Drain and as soon as it is cool enough to handle, squeeze dry with your hands and coarsely chop. Combine spinach, ricotta and butter. Add salt, pepper and nutmeg to taste. Set aside.

For bechamel, melt butter over medium heat in a heavy saucepan. Whisk in flour and cook until foaming, about 1 minute. Remove from heat and pour in milk gradually, whisking constantly. Return to heat and cook, whisking constantly, until sauce thickens, about 2 minutes. Bring to the boil and remove from heat. Add salt, pepper and nutmeg to taste.

Pour a thin layer of the bechamel just to cover the bottom of a 30cm x 20cm x 7.5cm (12in x 8in x 3in) buttered oven-proof dish. Lay 3 pasta sheets on top. Place one quarter of the spinach-ricotta mixture in an even layer onto the pasta. Pour over one quarter of the bechamel and sprinkle a quarter of the parmesan on top. Starting with another layer of 3 pasta sheets, repeat layers. Repeat layers again to finish, ending with parmesan. Bake until golden and bubbling, 20-30 minutes. Leave to stand for 5 minutes before serving.

WHICH PASTA?
Egg lasagne, fresh where possible.

COOKS' NOTE
We don't recommend no-cook lasagne, but if it is all you can find on the supermarket shelves, treat it as regular dried lasagne for this recipe and pre-cook until just pliable, about 30 seconds.

THINK AHEAD
Assemble lasagne and leave to cool completely. Cover, unbaked, and refrigerate up to 1 day in advance. Alternatively freeze, unbaked, up to 3 weeks in advance. Defrost overnight in refrigerator. Cook in preheated 200°C (400°F) Gas 6 oven for 30 minutes.
Make bechamel up to 2 days in advance. Cover with clingfilm, pressing down on the surface to prevent a skin forming. Refrigerate. Before using, return to room temperature and beat to make it easy to spread.

OTHER VEGETARIAN LASAGNES
SPINACH, GORGONZOLA AND PINE NUT LASAGNE

Have ready 200g (7oz) crumbled gorgonzola and 4 tbsp pine nuts. Assemble lasagne as directed, covering each layer of spinach-ricotta mixture with one quarter gorgonzola and 1 tbsp pine nuts before covering with bechamel and parmesan. Finish as directed.

AUBERGINE, BASIL AND MOZZARELLA LASAGNE

Omit spinach. Have ready 750g (1½lb) diced aubergine, 250g (8oz) grated mozzarella and 1 handful torn fresh basil. Spread aubergine pieces out in a roasting pan and drizzle over 3 tbsp extra virgin olive oil. Roast in a preheated 200°C (400°F) Gas 6 oven until soft, 20 minutes. Add salt and pepper to taste. Assemble lasagne as directed, covering each layer of pasta with one quarter ricotta, one quarter aubergine dice, one quarter grated mozzarella and one quarter torn basil before covering with bechamel and parmesan. Finish as directed.

MUSHROOM, GARLIC AND PARSLEY LASAGNE

Omit spinach. Have ready 750g (1½lb) sliced brown or wild mushrooms, 2 tbsp extra virgin olive oil, 3 finely chopped garlic cloves and 1 handful finely chopped fresh flat-leaf parsley. Heat oil in large frying pan. Add mushrooms and garlic and cook, stirring constantly, over medium-high heat until just coloured, 5 minutes. Add parsley and remove from heat. Add salt and pepper to taste. Assemble lasagne as directed, covering each layer of pasta with one quarter ricotta and one quarter mushroom mixture before covering with bechamel and parmesan. Finish as directed.

PASTA WITH BEANS AND LENTILS

BEANS AND LENTILS IN THE PASTA PANTRY

Although dried, all pulses should still have a fresh, unwrinkled look. Dried beans, chickpeas and lentils should be eaten within 12 months of being harvested, so renew your pantry supply yearly. If kept any longer they can become too dry and never cook properly until tender, however long you soak or boil them.

Chickpeas need soaking at least overnight and can take up to 4 hours to cook until tender. Luckily, tinned chickpeas are a perfectly good substitute for dried if well rinsed before using. If you can take the time, chickpeas are nicer skinned. Place cooked chickpeas in a bowl and cover with water. Gently rub the chickpeas between your fingers. The skins will slip off and float, while the chickpeas will sink. When you have finished, pour off the water and the skins together.

Lentils are an excellent pantry basic, as you don't have to soak them before cooking. For a truly Italian flavour, choose the small, brown Umbrian lentils which keep their shape when cooked. The very best are labelled Castelluccio; seek them out in good supermarkets and gourmet or Italian stores. Grey-green French puy lentils are a good substitute as they also hold their shape well when cooked.

Fresh green beans should be firm and crisp-looking. Look for green beans that are bright and snap readily when you bend them. Avoid any that are dull or limp. Buy fresh broad beans in the pod and choose smooth pods without wrinkled skins or blackened ends. The broad bean season is short, but small frozen beans are a good substitute. Unless very fresh and tender, broad beans are best skinned. Plunge into boiling water for 1 minute to loosen skins. Cool in cold water before draining and peeling.

QUICK COOK
CHICKPEAS WITH ROSEMARY, CHILLI AND GARLIC

SERVES 4

500g (1lb) dried pasta
6 tbsp extra virgin olive oil
4 garlic cloves, finely chopped
½ tsp crushed chilli flakes
2 tsp finely chopped fresh rosemary or
  1 tsp dried rosemary, crumbled
1- 400g (14oz) tin chickpeas, drained and rinsed
2 tbsp finely chopped fresh flat-leaf parsley
additional extra virgin olive oil
salt, black pepper

Cook pasta in a large pot of boiling, salted water, until firm to the bite. While pasta is cooking, heat oil in a large frying pan.

Add garlic, chilli flakes and rosemary and cook over medium-high heat until fragrant, 1 minute. Add chickpeas and cook until sizzling hot, 3 minutes. Drain pasta, reserving ½ cup pasta water. Add pasta with the parsley to the hot sauce. Toss well to coat, adding 2 tbsp additional olive oil, salt, pepper and reserved water as needed. Serve immediately.

WHICH PASTA?
Large tubes or shells - conchiglie, rigatoni, penne.

VARIATION
BROAD BEANS WITH PECORINO
Cook just 2 garlic cloves with chilli flakes as directed. Omit rosemary and chickpeas. Replace with 500g (1lb) frozen broad beans, defrosted and cooked with 3 tbsp water until beans are tender and water has evaporated, 3-5 minutes. Add drained pasta with 4 tbsp freshly grated pecorino to hot sauce. Finish as directed.

QUICK COOK
CLASSIC GENOESE PESTO

SERVES 4

125g (4oz) fine green beans
4 small new potatoes, sliced 0.25cm
  (⅛ in) thick
500g (1lb) dried pasta
1 recipe simple basil pesto
  (see page 105)
3 tbsp extra virgin olive oil
salt

Cook beans in a large pot of boiling salted water until tender, 5 minutes. Remove with a slotted spoon. Cool completely, by plunging into cold water, and reserve. Add potatoes to the pot and cook until tender in the centre when pierced with the tip of a small, sharp knife, 6-8 minutes. Remove with a slotted spoon and reserve. Add pasta to the pot and cook until firm to the bite if serving hot or just firm to the bite if serving as a salad. Return beans and potatoes to pot just before draining pasta, to heat through, 1 minute. Drain pasta, beans and potatoes, reserving ½ cup water. Return pasta, beans and potatoes with the pesto and olive oil to the warm pasta pot. Toss well, adding reserved water as needed. Add salt to taste. Serve immediately or at room temperature.

WHICH PASTA?
Strands or thin ribbons - linguine, trenette, spaghetti.

THINK AHEAD
Cook beans and potatoes up to 1 day in advance. Cool completely. Cover.
If serving as a salad, dress pasta up to 8 hours in advance. Cover and store at room temperature.

SLOW COOK
BRAISED UMBRIAN LENTILS

SERVES 4 - 6

300g (10oz) Umbrian or puy
  lentils
1 medium onion, cut in half
6 fresh sage leaves
2 fresh rosemary sprigs
1 tbsp salt
500g (1lb) dried pasta
4 fresh ripe tomatoes, peeled, seeded
  (see page 156) and chopped or
  4 tinned Italian plum tomatoes,
  chopped
2 garlic cloves, finely chopped
1 handful fresh flat-leaf parsley,
  chopped
5 tbsp extra virgin olive oil, plus
  additional for serving
freshly grated pecorino or parmesan

Place lentils, onion, sage, rosemary and salt in a large heavy-based pot. Cover with 3 litres (5 pints) cold water. Bring to a boil over a medium-high heat, stirring occasionally. Simmer gently until tender, 15-20 minutes. Bring water with lentils to a boil. Add pasta to pot and cook until pasta is just firm to the bite. Meanwhile, place tomatoes, garlic, parsley and oil in a large frying pan over medium-low heat. Cook until tomatoes soften, 3-4 minutes. When pasta is just firm to the bite, use a slotted spoon to transfer pasta and lentils to the pan, removing and discarding onion pieces and herbs. Turn heat to medium-high and cook, stirring constantly, 2-3 minutes. Serve immediately, with 5 tbsp additional olive oil and the grated cheese.

WHICH PASTA?
Shapes - conchiglie, gnocchi.

COOKS' NOTE
It is worth trying to find small, brown Umbrian lentils (see page 122). They give this dish an authentic flavour and texture.

PASTA WITH GARLIC

GARLIC IN THE PASTA PANTRY

When choosing garlic, look for firm, plump bulbs. Cloves that are shrivelled will be dry with a musty, slightly metallic taste. Before chopping, we advise cutting garlic cloves in half and removing the inner green stem, as it has a slightly bitter flavour. New season fresh garlic is sweet and tender and can be used liberally.

For only a hint of garlic flavour, peel a clove of garlic, cut in half and cook in the butter or oil, removing and discarding when golden. Some cooks put a wooden toothpick through the garlic clove so it can be spotted easily and removed whenever it has released enough flavour.

When frying garlic, take care not to let it burn because it will give a bitter taste to the sauce.

Store garlic in a cool, dark place. The simplest way to peel garlic is to crush it with the flat side of a large knife (see page 156).

QUICK COOK
OLIO AGLIO

SERVES 4
500g (1lb) dried pasta
8 tbsp extra virgin olive oil
4 garlic cloves, finely chopped
salt, black pepper

Cook pasta in a large pot of boiling, salted water, until firm to the bite. While pasta is cooking, heat oil in a large frying pan. Add garlic and cook, stirring occasionally over medium heat until golden, 2 minutes. Add salt and pepper to taste. Drain pasta. Add drained pasta to oil and garlic in the pan. Toss well to coat. Serve immediately.

WHICH PASTA?
Strands - spaghetti, spaghettini.

VARIATIONS
OLIO AGLIO PEPERONCINO
Add ½ tsp crushed chilli flakes with garlic. Finish as directed.

OLIVE OIL, GARLIC AND PARSLEY
Add 3 tbsp chopped fresh flat-leaf parsley with garlic. Finish as directed.

OLIVE OIL, GARLIC AND FRESH TOMATO
Add 3 ripe fresh tomatoes, peeled, seeded (see page 156) and chopped with garlic. Finish as directed.

ROAST GARLIC AND CHERRY TOMATOES

SERVES 4

1kg (2lb) cherry tomatoes, halved
16 garlic cloves, peeled
8 tbsp extra virgin olive oil
¼ tsp crushed chilli flakes
½ tsp salt
¼ tsp black pepper
500g (1lb) dried pasta
1 handful torn fresh basil leaves

Preheat oven to 200°C (400°F) Gas 6. Arrange tomatoes and garlic cloves so that they fit snugly in an oven tray or oven-proof pan. Drizzle with oil and sprinkle with chilli flakes, salt and pepper. Roast until garlic is soft and golden, 25 minutes.

Meanwhile, cook pasta in a large pot of boiling, salted water, until firm to the bite. Drain. Return pasta with tomatoes and garlic to the warm pasta pot. Toss well to coat. Sprinkle with basil. Serve immediately.

WHICH PASTA?
Strands - spaghettini, spaghetti.

THINK AHEAD
Roast tomatoes and garlic up to 1 day in advance. Cover and refrigerate. Reheat in preheated 200°C (400°F) Gas 6 oven for 10 minutes.

SLOW COOK
GOLDEN GARLIC AND ONION

SERVES 4

60g (2oz) butter
3 tbsp extra virgin olive oil
8 garlic cloves, finely chopped
1lb (500g) onions, finely sliced
1 tsp sugar
salt
8 tbsp dry white wine
175ml (6floz) double cream
black pepper
500g (1lb) dried pasta
4 tbsp freshly grated parmesan,
  plus additional to serve

Melt butter and oil in a heavy-based pot over low heat. Add garlic, onion, sugar and 1 tsp salt. Cover and cook gently, stirring occasionally, until very soft, 30 minutes. Add 1 or 2 tbsp hot water to pan if necessary to prevent browning. Uncover and turn the heat to medium-high. Add wine and simmer until just evaporated, 2 minutes. Stir in the cream. Heat through and simmer until just thickened, 1-2 minutes. Add salt and pepper to taste. Meanwhile, cook pasta in a large pot of boiling, salted water, until firm to the bite. Drain and add pasta with parmesan to the hot sauce. Toss well to coat. Serve immediately with additional parmesan.

WHICH PASTA?
Strands or medium ribbons - spaghetti, paglia e fieno, fettuccine, tagliatelle.

THINK AHEAD
Make sauce up to 4 days in advance, omitting the cream. Cool sauce completely. Cover and refrigerate. Reheat and add cream just before serving. Finish as directed.

COOK'S NOTE
This is one of the traditional sauces from Emilia Romagna. Garlic is used very sparingly in this region. But we find that, being cooked for a long time, its flavour mellows and combines well with the onion.

VARIATION
GOLDEN GARLIC, ONION AND FENNEL

Reduce the quantity of onions to 250g (8oz). Add 1 finely chopped large fennel bulb to the pan with the garlic, onions, sugar and salt. Cook and finish sauce as directed.

PASTA WITH PEPPERS AND AUBERGINES

PEPPERS AND AUBERGINES IN THE PASTA PANTRY

Choose aubergines with smooth, glossy and unblemished skins. There is no need to salt and de-gorge aubergines before using. The bitter juices that made this process essential in the past have been bred out of most modern aubergine varieties.

Peppers should be shiny, firm and crisp, with no wrinkles. Hold a pepper in your hand before buying. The heavier the pepper, the better it is, as it will have meatier and juicier flesh. Colour is an indication of ripeness, so, for optimum sweetness, choose the deepest red peppers.

Roasting and peeling peppers is well worth the extra effort. Roasting peppers brings out their flavour, while peeling removes the papery, indigestible skin.

Roast whole peppers under a hot grill, turning as needed until charred and wrinkled on all sides, 10-15 minutes. Wrap in a plastic bag or place in a bowl with a plate on top and leave until cool. The steam released by the peppers as they cool will loosen the skin.

To peel, remove pepper from bag or bowl. Peel off the charred skin, using the tip of a small knife. Scrape rather than rinse off any remaining bits of skin; rinsing washes away flavour. You can roast and peel peppers up to a week in advance. Cover with oil and refrigerate.

Although ready roast peppers in jars are a quick substitute for fresh roast peppers, they never really lose their distinctive "jar" taste.

QUICK COOK
ROAST PEPPER

SERVES 4

4 red peppers
6 tbsp extra virgin olive oil
2 garlic cloves, finely chopped
½ tsp crushed chilli flakes
salt, black pepper
500g (1lb) dried pasta
3 tbsp chopped fresh flat-leaf parsley
additional olive oil, optional

Grill, peel and seed peppers (see page 157). Cut into strips 5cm (2in) long and 1cm (½in) wide. Heat oil in a large frying pan. Add garlic and chilli flakes and cook over medium-high heat until fragrant, 1 minute. Add peppers and cook, stirring occasionally, until flavours are blended, 4 minutes. Add salt and pepper to taste. Meanwhile, cook pasta in a large pot of boiling, salted water, until firm to the bite. Drain. Add drained pasta with parsley to the hot peppers. Toss well. Drizzle with additional olive oil, if using. Serve immediately.

WHICH PASTA?
Large tubes - penne, rigatoni.

QUICK COOK
AUBERGINE WITH CHILLI AND GARLIC

SERVES 4

7 tbsp extra virgin olive oil
400g (14oz) aubergines, cut into 1cm (½ in) dice
4 garlic cloves, crushed
½ tsp crushed chilli flakes
2 tbsp tomato purée
1 tsp dried oregano
salt, black pepper
500g (1lb) dried pasta
additional olive oil to toss

Heat oil in a large frying pan. Add aubergine, garlic and chilli flakes and cook, stirring frequently over high heat, until golden, 5-7 minutes. Turn down heat to medium-low. Stir in tomato purée and oregano and cook, stirring occasionally, until aubergine dice are soft and cooked through, 10 minutes. Add 2 tbsp hot water to the pan if the aubergine begins to stick. Add salt and pepper to taste. Meanwhile, cook pasta in a large pot of boiling, salted water, until firm to the bite. Drain. Add pasta with 2 tbsp additional olive oil to the hot sauce. Toss well to coat. Serve immediately.

WHICH PASTA?
Tubes or shapes - penne, rigatoni, orecchiette, conchiglie, fusilli.

COOKS' NOTE
To enhance the flavour of the spicy chilli flakes with the aubergine, we like to use a slightly peppery Tuscan or Pugliese olive oil.

VARIATIONS
SICILIAN AUBERGINE WITH GARLIC
Add 2 tbsp capers and 10 sliced pitted black olives with the tomato purée and oregano. Finish as directed.

AUBERGINE WITH MOLTEN MOZZARELLA
Make sauce as directed. Stir 250g (8oz) diced mozzarella into the finished sauce and heat gently until just melting, 1 minute. Add drained pasta to the hot sauce, omitting the additional olive oil. Finish as directed.

SPICY AUBERGINE WITH GARLIC, BASIL AND PINE NUTS
Make sauce as directed. Add the drained pasta with 2 tbsp pine nuts and 1 handful torn fresh basil to the hot sauce.

AUBERGINE WITH GARLIC AND RICOTTA
Make sauce as directed. Stir 125g (4oz) crumbled ricotta into the finished sauce and heat gently until warm through, 1 minute. Add drained pasta with 3 tbsp freshly grated pecorino to the hot sauce, omitting the additional olive oil.

ROAST VEGETABLES WITH GREEN OLIVES AND RICOTTA

SERVES 4

1 aubergine, cut into 1cm (½in) cubes
1 red or yellow pepper, cut into 1cm (½in) pieces
1 small fennel bulb, cut into 1cm (½in) pieces
4 ripe tomatoes, cut into quarters
6 whole garlic cloves, peeled
½ tsp crushed chilli flakes
5 tbsp extra virgin olive oil
salt, black pepper
500g (1lb) dried pasta
additional extra virgin olive oil for tossing
125g (4oz) pitted green olives
125g (4oz) ricotta, crumbled
1 handful fresh basil leaves
freshly grated parmesan to serve

Preheat oven to 200°C (400°F) Gas 6. Toss aubergine, red or yellow pepper, fennel, tomatoes and garlic with chilli flakes and oil to coat well. Spread out on a baking tray. Sprinkle with salt and pepper. Roast until soft and lightly charred, 20-25 minutes. Meanwhile, cook pasta in a large pot of boiling, salted water, until firm to the bite. Drain. Return drained pasta to the warm pasta pot and toss in 2 tbsp additional olive oil. Add roasted vegetables to pasta and toss well to coat. Add olives, ricotta and basil. Serve immediately with parmesan.

WHICH PASTA?
Medium tubes - macaroni, pennette, ditali.

THINK AHEAD
Roast vegetables up to 1 day in advance. Cover and refrigerate. Reheat in 200°C (400°F) Gas 6 oven for 10 minutes before tossing with cooked pasta.

RED PEPPER PESTO

SERVES 4

2 large red peppers
2 garlic cloves
5 tbsp pine nuts, preferably toasted (see page 161)
¼ tsp crushed chilli flakes
½ tsp balsamic vinegar
5 tbsp extra virgin olive oil
salt, black pepper
500g (1lb) dried pasta
freshly grated parmesan to serve

Roast, peel and seed peppers (see page 157). Place peppers, garlic, pine nuts, chilli flakes, vinegar and oil in a food processor; pulse until smooth. Add salt and pepper to taste. Meanwhile, cook pasta in a large pot of boiling, salted water, until firm to the bite. Drain, reserving ½ cup pasta water. Return drained pasta to the warm pasta pot and add red pepper pesto. Toss well to coat, adding reserved water as needed. Serve immediately with parmesan.

WHICH PASTA?
Strands or tubes - spaghetti, spaghettini, penne.

THINK AHEAD
Make pesto up to 3 days in advance. Cover and refrigerate.

SLOW COOK
ROAST PEPPER AND TOMATO SAUCE

SERVES 4

2 red peppers
6 tbsp extra virgin olive oil
1 garlic clove, crushed
¼ tsp crushed chilli flakes
6 tomatoes, peeled, seeded
  (see page 156) and chopped
salt, black pepper
500g (1lb) dried pasta

Roast, peel and seed peppers (see page 157) and finely chop. Heat oil in a large frying pan. Add garlic and chilli flakes and cook over medium heat until fragrant, 1 minute. Add tomatoes and cook, stirring occasionally, until thick, 20 minutes. Add peppers and cook to heat through and blend flavours, 5-10 minutes. Add salt and pepper to taste. Meanwhile, cook pasta in a large pot of boiling, salted water, until firm to the bite. Drain. Add drained pasta to the hot sauce. Toss well to coat. Serve immediately.

WHICH PASTA?
Strands or tubes - spaghetti, penne, ditali.

THINK AHEAD
Make sauce up to 3 days in advance. Cover and refrigerate.

COOKS' NOTE
A peppery Tuscan olive oil will enhance - and stand up to - the flavour of this lively, gutsy pasta sauce.

SLOW COOK
ROAST VEGETABLES AL FORNO

SERVES 4

1 aubergine, cut into 1cm (½in) dice
2 red peppers, cut into 1cm (½in) dice
2 garlic cloves, crushed
¼ tsp crushed chilli flakes
3 tbsp extra virgin olive oil
salt, black pepper
500g (1lb) dried pasta
1 recipe simmered tomato
  sauce (see page 42)
125g (4oz) ricotta, crumbled
125g (4oz) mozzarella, sliced
6 tbsp freshly grated parmesan

Preheat oven to 200°C (400°F) Gas 6. Toss the aubergine and pepper pieces with garlic, chilli flakes and oil to coat well. Spread out evenly on a baking tray. Sprinkle with salt and pepper.

Roast until soft and lightly charred, 20-25 minutes. Meanwhile, cook pasta in a large pot of boiling, salted water, until just firm to the bite. Drain pasta and combine with with tomato sauce and roasted vegetables. Toss well to coat. Add salt and pepper to taste. Place half tossed pasta in an oiled 20cm x 20cm x 5cm (8in x 8in x 2in) oven-proof dish. Cover with ricotta, mozzarella and half the parmesan. Top with remaining pasta. Sprinkle with remaining parmesan. Bake until golden and bubbling, 10 minutes. Leave to stand for 5 minutes before serving.

WHICH PASTA?
Large tubes or shells - rigatoni, penne, conchiglie.

THINK AHEAD
Assemble, cover unbaked and refrigerate up to 8 hours in advance. Alternatively, cover unbaked and freeze up to 3 weeks in advance. Defrost overnight in refrigerator. Cook in preheated 200°C (400°F) Gas 6 oven for 30 minutes.

FRESH & FILLED PASTA

FRESH EGG PASTA

SERVES 4

300g (10oz) italian 00 (doppio zero) or plain flour
½ tsp salt
3 eggs
additional flour for dusting

ESSENTIAL EQUIPMENT
pasta machine

Mix the flour and salt into a bowl. Make a well in the centre of the flour. Add eggs to the well. With a fork, beat the eggs and gradually draw in the flour. With your hands, mix in as much of the flour as needed to make a rough dough. You may not need to incorporate all of the flour. Or if the dough is too sticky, you may need to sprinkle over a little extra flour.

As soon as the dough begins to form a ball, turn it out onto a work surface lightly dusted with flour.

Knead the dough by pushing it away from you with the heel of your hand. Knead until smooth, elastic and no longer sticky, 10 minutes. Wrap in clingfilm and leave to rest for at least 30 minutes or up to 4 hours.

COOKS' NOTE
The finest fresh pasta is always made at home. Homemade fresh pasta is simple, fun and very satisfying to make. We advise making fresh pasta by hand rather than in a food processor. Eggs vary in size and different flours will absorb different quantities of liquid on different days, depending on whether you are working in a dry or humid atmosphere. It's always easier to add more flour to a dough that is too soft than correct a dough that is too stiff. Working by hand allows you to adjust the quantity of flour as you go along.

ROLLING OUT FRESH PASTA

Set the pasta machine rollers on their widest setting. Cut the dough into 4 equal-sized pieces. Lightly dust 1 piece of dough with flour and flatten with your hand. Keep the remaining pieces wrapped in clingfilm. Feed 1 piece pasta dough through the rollers. Place the rolled strip flat on the table and fold in half. Feed the folded dough through the rollers again. Give the dough a quarter turn before feeding it each time through the machine, to ensure that it is evenly kneaded. Repeat folding and rolling out 5 or 6 times until the dough is smooth and silky. Reset the rollers to the next setting and feed the dough through the settings until you achieve the desired thickness (see below for tagliatelle, tagliolini or lasagne; see page 146 for ravioli). If the dough sticks to the machine, dust both sides lightly with flour.

THINK AHEAD
Make, roll and cut dough up to 5 days in advance. Leave to dry out, then store at room temperature in single layers on paper towels set over a tray. Cover with a clean tea towel. Alternatively, freeze for up to 4 months. Leave to dry out, then place in freezer bags or an airtight container. Freeze.

FRESH TAGLIATELLE OR TAGLIOLINI
Roll the dough through the machine on the second to thinnest setting. Lay each pasta sheet on a clean tea towel, letting about one third of its length hang down over the edge of the work surface. Leave until the pasta is dry to the touch but still pliable, about 10–30 minutes. Feed each sheet of dough through the broad cutters of the machine for tagliatelle or through the narrow ones for tagliolini.
As the strips emerge, catch them on your hand. Sprinkle with a little semolina or plain flour, then coil loosely into a bundle. Place on a clean tea towel and repeat with remaining dough. The pasta strands are now ready to be cooked. Alternatively, place in a single layer on clean tea towels until dry, about 24 hours.

FRESH LASAGNE
Roll out the dough on the last setting of the machine. Cut each pasta sheet into squares about 12 x 8.5cm (5 x 3½in). Cook immediately or leave to dry as for tagliatelle or tagliolini.

FRESH RAVIOLI

SERVES 4

1 recipe pasta dough (see page 144)
1 recipe pasta filling (see page 147)
plain flour or semolina for dusting

ESSENTIAL EQUIPMENT
pasta machine, pastry brush, fluted
pastry wheel

Roll the dough through the machine on
the second to thinnest setting (see page
145). Cut the dough sheets into 50cm
(20in) lengths. Cover the dough sheets
with clingfilm to keep them pliable until
you are ready to shape them.

Fold the sheet in half to make a crease
down the centre. Unfold. Using the
crease as a guide, place teaspoonfuls
of the filling at 4cm (1½in) intervals in
2 rows along opposite sides of the crease.
Lightly brush the pasta around the filling
with water. Lay over a second pasta
sheet to cover the filling. With your
fingertips, press gently around each
mound of filling to seal the dough and
to push out any pockets of air. Cut into
squares with a fluted pastry wheel.

Place the squares upside down on a
clean tea towel, making sure they do not
touch. Repeat with remaining dough.
The ravioli are now ready to be cooked.
Alternatively, leave to dry on clean tea
towels, turning over occasionally, until
the dough has dried out completely,
about 24 hours.

Cook the ravioli in gently boiling,
salted water under tender to the bite,
4-7 minutes. To drain, scoop out with a
slotted spoon and shake off excess water.
Place in a warmed bowl and toss gently
to coat with sauce. Serve immediately.

THINK AHEAD
Make ravioli up to 3 days in advance. Leave to dry
out, then store on layers of greaseproof paper in an
airtight container in the refrigerator. Alternatively,
freeze for up to 2 months. Spread ravioli in a single
layer on a baking sheet, making sure that the
edges are not touching. Place in freezer uncovered
until hard, 30 minutes. Once the ravioli are frozen,
pack into zip-lock bags or an airtight container and
return to the freezer. Frozen ravioli should be
cooked from frozen, allowing an extra 5 minutes
of cooking time.

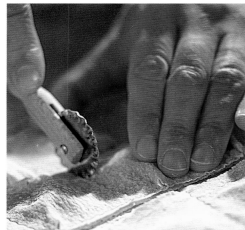

GREENS, PARMESAN AND RICOTTA FILLING

SERVES 4

1kg (2lb) spinach or swiss chard,
  washed and stemmed
250g (8oz) ricotta
8 tbsp freshly grated parmesan
salt, pepper, nutmeg
2 eggs

Wash but do not dry spinach. Place wet spinach in a covered pan over a medium heat. Cook, stirring occasionally, until tender, 5 minutes. Drain and leave to cool. Squeeze out excess water with your hands. Chop finely and combine with ricotta and parmesan. Add salt, pepper and nutmeg to taste. Add eggs and mix to a stiff paste.

WHICH SAUCE?
Sizzling Sage Butter (see page 108), Butter and Parmesan (see page 47), Fresh Tomato (see page 37).

VARIATIONS

RICOTTA AND HERB FILLING

Replace spinach with 2 handfuls chopped fresh basil or parsley. Combine basil or parsley with ricotta and parmesan. Finish as directed.

PORCINI MUSHROOM FILLING

SERVES 4

25g (1oz) dried porcini mushrooms
3 tbsp olive oil
2 garlic cloves, finely chopped
1 shallot, finely chopped
625g (20oz) brown or field
  mushrooms, finely chopped
2 tbsp finely chopped fresh
  flat-leaf parsley

Soak porcini (see page 156) and finely chop. Heat oil in a large frying pan. Add garlic and shallots and cook over medium-high heat until fragrant, 1 minute. Add mushrooms and porcini and cook, stirring frequently, until crisp, 10 minutes. Add parsley and salt and pepper to taste. Leave to cool completely before using to fill ravioli.

WHICH SAUCE?
Fresh Tomato (see page 37), Butter and Parmesan (see page 47), All'Alfredo (see page 53).

THINK AHEAD
Make fillings up to 1 day in advance. Cover and refrigerate.

147

THINK AHEAD TIPS

COOKING PASTA FOR A BAKED DISH

When cooking pasta for a dish that will require further cooking, such as baked or layered pasta, the cooking time should be cut by approximately a third. Depending on the kind of pasta you are cooking, this means you should begin checking for doneness (see page 23) a couple of minutes early. Remove and drain the pasta when it is still slightly hard at the centre.

PREPARING AN UNBAKED PASTA DISH FOR THE FREEZER

When preparing baked pasta dishes, such as lasagne, ahead of time, you will get better results if you prepare the dish and freeze it before baking.

If you wish to use the casserole dish while the assembled dish is stored in the freezer, line the casserole dish with heavy-duty aluminium foil, allowing enough foil to come over the sides of the dish to cover and seal the food.

Assemble the dish. Be sure that all the ingredients in the assembled dish are at room temperature before placing it in the freezer.

Do not cover the top with the extended foil at the sides. Freeze until solid, then use the sides to lift the frozen dish out of the casserole. Cover the frozen dish with the foil sides to seal. Place in a large zip-lock freezer bag and return to the freezer until ready to use.

DEFROSTING AN UNBAKED PASTA DISH

Remove from freezer bag and place the frozen dish in the casserole in which it will be baked. Place in the refrigerator and allow the dish to thaw overnight, before baking.

DEFROSTING AND REHEATING PASTA SAUCES

Allow frozen pasta sauces to thaw overnight in the refrigerator.

When reheating a sauce, especially in the case of one that has been previously frozen, additional liquid will in most cases be needed to return the sauce to the proper consistency.

In the case of rich cream-based or meat sauces, use a few tablespoons of warm milk to add moisture and to retain the rich flavour. In the case of olive oil and tomato based sauces, remember to reserve about half a cup of the pasta water before draining the pasta. Use this, or part of it, to add both moisture and flavour back to the reheated sauce.

MAKING AND FREEZING PASTA SAUCES

Be sure that the sauce has cooled completely before storing it in the freezer.

Choose a container for freezing that has a capacity as close to the actual volume of the sauce prepared as possible. The more oxygen permitted to surround frozen food, the greater the chance of freezer burn and spoilage.

The best way to freeze anything is in a zip-lock freezer bag. Transfer the cooled sauce to a zip-lock freezer bag, expelling as much air as possible before sealing it. Place on a plate until frozen solid then remove the plate.

PASTA IN THE PANTRY

Fast food doesn't have to mean take-away when you have pasta in the pantry. Perfect for impromptu entertaining, pasta is the original convenience food. A well-stocked pantry is the key. With a few well-chosen staples (see below) in the kitchen cupboard, refrigerator or freezer, a simple meal can be on the table in the time it takes to boil water.

To save you scanning the index, we've compiled an easy reference **PASTA PLANNER** (see pages 152-153) that cross-refers ingredients with cooking time. You can select recipes at a glance, simply by matching your schedule to the contents of your shopping basket or pantry.

Pasta is unquestionably the most versatile of foods. It is an everyday food and a food for celebrations. It makes a last-minute supper for one and a satisfying meal for all the family. Refer to **PASTA ON THE MENU** (see pages 154-155) and you'll see that, whatever the season, the occasion, the time available or the cook's mood, pasta will serve.

IN THE REFRIGERATOR

PARMESAN
Buy in a piece and store in the warmest section of the refrigerator.

BUTTER
Must be unsalted for pasta sauces.

EGGS
Buy large and choose organic when possible.

CREAM
For cooking, choose double cream or crème fraîche. Crème fraîche is a great pantry basic as it keeps longer than regular cream.

LEMONS
Buy organic lemons when possible, but especially when the recipe calls for grated lemon zest, as organic lemons are not waxed or sprayed with chemicals.

IN THE FREEZER

UNSMOKED PANCETTA
Cut and wrap in 60g (2oz) pieces. Unsmoked streaky bacon is an acceptable alternative.

FROZEN PEAS
Choose tiny, young *petits pois* when possible.

PARSLEY
Buy a bunch of flat-leaf parsley, chop and keep in an airtight container for using as needed.

In the Cupboard

DRIED PASTA
Have a selection of shapes and a variety of sizes on hand.

ANCHOVIES
Buy in tins or jars. Alternatively, have a tube of anchovy paste in the refrigerator (see page 160).

TUNA
Choose tins of tuna packed in olive oil for best texture and taste. We prefer yellowfin and bonito to skipjack.

TOMATOES
Choose tins of Italian brands for tastier, juicier tomatoes.

CAPERS
Buy in jars, in brine or salt (see page 160).

OLIVES
Black are the most useful in the pasta pantry.

CRUSHED CHILLI FLAKES
Renew your supply yearly as dried chilli loses its kick over time.

DRIED PORCINI
Buy packets with large pieces, which are from the mushroom caps. The smaller, crumblier pieces come from the stalks and have less flavour.

ONIONS
Small yellow onions are the most useful.

WHITE WINE
Choose a dry, light white wine.

GARLIC
Choose milder pink-skinned garlic when possible.

OLIVE OIL
Always buy extra virgin. We like to have a regular brand on hand for cooking, plus a bottle of premium oil for seasoning and drizzling.

COARSE SALT
Sea salt is the choice of all food lovers because of its fuller flavour.

BLACK PEPPERCORNS
Always buy whole peppercorns and freshly grind to order.

PASTA PLANNER

	MAKE AHEAD	NO COOK	QUICK COOK	SLOW COOK	AL FORNO
ASPARAGUS			• Asparagus with Cream • Asparagus, Prosciutto & Fresh Herbs		
AUBERGINE			• Aubergine with Chilli & Garlic	• Roast Vegetables with Green Olives & Ricotta	• RoastVegetables al Forno
BASIL	• Simple Basil Pesto	• Simple Basil Pesto • Even Simpler Basil Pesto • Lemon, Basil & Mascarpone	• Classic Genoese Pesto		
BEEF	• Classic Ragù Bolognese • Lasagne Al Forno		• Pizzaiola	• Classic Ragù Bolognese	• Lasagne al Forno
BROCCOLI			• Spicy Broccoli		
BUTTER		• Butter & Parmesan			
CHICKEN	• Chicken, Tomato & Rosemary Ragù		• Pan-Roast Chicken with Lemon & Mushrooms	• Chicken, Tomato & Rosemary Ragù	
CREAM		• Cream & Parmesan	• Golden Saffron • All'Alfredo		
GARLIC			• Olio Aglio • Roast Garlic & Cherry Tomatoes	• Golden Garlic & Onion	
GORGONZOLA	• 4 cheese	• Gorgonzola & Ricotta	• Gorgonzola Cream		• 4 Cheese
MOZZARELLA	• 4 Cheese • Tomato and Mozzarella al Forno	• 3 Cheese • Fresh Tomato with Mozzarella	• Fresh Tomato Sauce with Molten Mozzarella • Pan-Cooked Tomato & Mozzarella	• Tomato & Mozzarella Al Forno	• Tomato and Mozzarella al Forno
MUSHROOMS	• Mushroom al Forno		• Wild Mushroom Persillade • Mushroom, White Wine & Cream		• Mushroom al Forno
DRIED PORCINI	• Tomato with Porcini		• Porcini, White Wine & Cream		• Mushroom al Forno
OLIVES	• Chilli Olive Pesto • Olive, Anchovy & Caper Pesto	• Chilli Olive Pesto • Olive, Anchovy & Caper Pesto	• Spicy Lemon Olive • Puttanesca		
PANCETTA			• Carbonara • Crispy Pancetta with Spring Onions • Amatriciana		

	MAKE AHEAD	NO COOK	QUICK COOK	SLOW COOK	AL FORNO
PARSLEY	• Parsley Pesto	• Parsley Pesto • Butter, Parmesan & Parsley	• Fresh Fragrant Herbs		
PEAS	• Primavera		• Peas, Prosciutto & Fresh Herbs • Primavera • Butter, Parmesan & Peas		
PEPPERS	• Roast Vegetables al Forno • Red Pepper Pesto • Roast Pepper & Tomato Sauce		• Roast Vegetables with Green Olives & Ricotta • Red Pepper Pesto	• Roast Pepper & Tomato Sauce	• Roast Vegetables al Forno
PRAWNS	• Prawns with Lemon & Basil	• Prawns with Lemon & Basil	• Spicy Garlic Prawns with Cherry Tomatoes • Chilli Prawns		
PROSCIUTTO			• Prosciutto & Cream • Peas, Prosciutto & Fresh Herbs		
SAUSAGE	• Spicy Sausage Ragù		• Sausage with Cream & Basil	• Spicy Sausage Ragù	
SPINACH	• Spinach & Walnut Pesto • Spinach & Ricotta Lasagne	• Spinach & Walnut Pesto	• Wilted Spinach with Golden Garlic	• Spinach & Ricotta Lasagne	• Spinach & Ricotta Lasagne
SMOKED SALMON		• Smoked Salmon, Vodka & Dill	• Smoked Salmon with White Wine, Cream & Chives		
TOMATOES Fresh	• Puttanesca • Arrabbiata • Napolitana • Roast Tomato		• Fresh Tomato • Puttanesca • Arrabbiata • Napolitana	• Roast Tomato	
Sun-dried	• Red Pesto • Sun-dried Tomato with Chilli, Garlic and Black Olives	• Red Pesto			
Tinned	• Puttanesca • Arrabbiata • Napolitana • Tomato & Mozzarella al Forno • Simmered Tomato		• Puttanesca • Arrabbiata • Napolitana • Pan-Cooked Tomato & Mozzarella	• Tomato & Mozzarella al Forno • Simmered Tomato	• Tomato & Mozzarella al Forno
TUNA	• Tuna with Lemon & Capers • Tuna & Tomato	• Tuna with Lemom & Capers	• Tuna & Tomato		

PASTA ON THE MENU

SHORT ORDER PASTA

In a rush? Try these fast and simple sauces, based on a few fresh ingredients, that are on the table in less than 20 minutes.

Butter, Parmesan & Asparagus
(See page 47)
Scallops with Garlic &
Crisp Crumbs
(See page 68)
Chicken with Lemon &
Mushrooms
(See page 87)
Lemon, Basil & Mascarpone
(See page 51)
Fresh Tomato Sauce with
Molten Mozzarella
(See page 37)
Smoked Salmon with
Vodka & Dill
(See page 64)
Pizzaiola
(See page 83)

PASTA TO CELEBRATE SPRING

Winter is finally over and the season's first fresh roots and shoots appear on the market. Why not celebrate, Italian-style?

Peas, Prosciutto & Fresh Herbs
(See page 111)
Primavera
(See page 116)
Broad Beans with Pecorino
(See page 123)
Parsley Pesto
(See page 107)
Asparagus with Cream
(See page 112)

PASTA SOLO

There's no need to go without because it's just you at home this evening. Treat yourself! Pasta makes cooking for one fun.

Olio Aglio
(See page 129)
Even Simpler Basil Pesto
(See page 105)
Three Cheese
(See page 49)
Salmon Caviar with
Butter & Chives
(See page 66)
Butter & Parmesan
(See page 47)
Fresh Herbs &
Golden Crumbs
(See page 108)

SELF-SERVE PASTA FOR A BUFFET OUTDOORS

Light, fresh and mayo-free, our pasta salads are more truly Italian than patio cuisine. Try one out and see, but we're confident you'll be converted!

Fresh Tomato, Rocket &
Balsamic Vinegar
(See page 33)
Tuna with Lemon & Capers
(See page 64)
Classic Genoese Pesto
(See page 124)
Sun-Dried Tomato with Chilli,
Garlic & Black Olives
(See page 33)

PASTA FOR CHILDREN

Even babies in highchairs love pasta. Try these dishes out on young mouths: they'll soon be firm favourites with all the family.

Simmered Tomato
(See page 42)
Butter, Parmesan & Peas
(See page 47)
Four Cheese Al Forno
(See page 52)
Tuna and Tomato
(See page 69)
Classic Ragù Bolognese
(See page 91)
Napolitana
(See page 35)

DO-AHEAD DINNER PARTY PASTA

Many pasta sauces can be prepared well in advance. Any of these simple recipes will make an elegant opener for six or a non-meat main for four. Refer to our Think Ahead notes.

Spinach & Walnut Pesto
(See page 107)
Simmered Tomato
with Vodka
(See page 42)
Primavera with Cream
(See page 116)
Roast Vegetables with
Green Olives & Ricotta
(See page 138)
Roast Tomato with Pesto
(See page 40)

COLD WEATHER COMFORT PASTA

When the sky's grey and the wind bites, nothing beats a steaming bowl of pasta for lighting up faces around the table.

Spicy Sausage Ragù
(See page 91)
Golden Garlic & Onion
(See page 131)
Braised Umbrian Lentils
(See page 124)
Ragù Al Forno
(See page 92)
Pan-Cooked Tomato & Mozzarella
(See page 39)

IMPROMPTU PASTA

With our well-chosen staples on hand (refer to Pasta in the Pantry on page 150) even the busiest of cooks can create a quick-fix meal in a matter of minutes.

Tuna & Tomato
(See page 69)
All'Alfredo
(See page 53)
Olio Aglio Peperoncino
(See page 129)
Tomatoes with Porcini
(See page 60)
Butter, Parmesan & Peas
(See page 47)
Spicy Lemon Olive
(See page 101)

PASTA ITALIA

Simple, honest, traditional dishes full of the charm and flavour of Italy.

Napolitana
(See page 35)
Carbonara
(See page 88)
Arrabbiata
(See page 35)
Puttanesca
(See page 34)
Olio Aglio Peperoncino
(See page 129)
Amatriciana
(See page 87)

PASTA TO IMPRESS

Here is a repertoire of simple but stylish pasta dishes that make you look good, whether you're out to impress friends, family, your boss or your date!

Spicy Garlic Prawns with Cherry Tomatoes
(See page 73)
Pan-Roast Chicken with Garlic & Shallots
(See page 84)
Seafood Extravaganza
(See page 77)
Scallops with Creme Fraiche & Dill
(See page 72)
Smoked Salmon with White Wine, Cream & Chives
(See page 70)
Wild Mushroom Persillade
(See page 57)

PASTA FOR CROWDS

Easy and economical, pasta can feed hoards of hungry mouths, without breaking the bank or causing sleepless nights. Refer to our Think Ahead notes.

Spinach & Ricotta Lasagne
(See page 118)
Mushroom Al Forno
(See page 60)
Tomato & Mozzarella Al Forno
(See page 39)
Roast Vegetables Al Forno
(See page 141)
Classic Lasagne Al Forno
(See page 95)

SUMMER WEEKEND PASTA

Light dishes with bright tastes for lazy lunches in the sunshine.

Fresh Tomato Sauce with Pesto
(See page 37)
Aubergine with Garlic, Basil & Pine Nuts
(See page 137)
Chilli Prawns
(See page 70)
Fresh Tomato, Red Onion & Basil
(See page 33)
Red Pesto with Rocket
(See page 31)
Spicy Garlic Scallops
(See page 73)

THE SKILLS - TOP TIPS

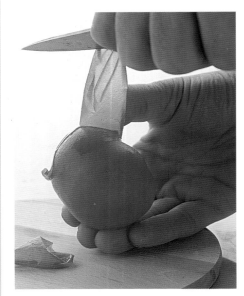

PEELING TOMATOES
Cut a small cross on the base of each tomato. Drop tomatoes into boiling water. Remove when you see the edges of the cross begin to loosen, 10-20 seconds, depending on the ripeness. Drain, then immerse tomatoes in cold water. Peel off the loosened skins, using the tip of a knife.

SOAKING DRIED MUSHROOMS
Place mushrooms in a small bowl and add boiling water to cover. Leave for 30 minutes.

SEEDING TOMATOES
Cut the tomato in half crosswise. Gently squeeze each tomato half, pushing out the seeds with your fingertips.

PEELING A GARLIC CLOVE
Set the flat side of the knife on top and strike it with your fist. This action will loosen the skin, allowing it to peel away easily. Discard the skin.

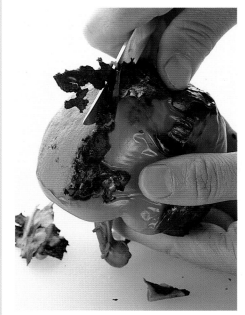

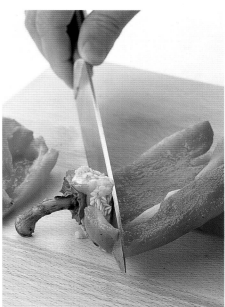

CHOPPING AN ONION

Peel the onion, leaving the root end on. Cut the onion in half and lay one half, cut side down, on a chopping board. With a sharp knife, cut horizontally towards the root end, and then vertically. Be sure to cut just to the root but not through it. Finally, cut the onion crosswise into diced pieces.

PEELING PEPPERS

Grill peppers under a preheated grill. Turn as needed until blackened on all sides, 10-15 minutes. Place in a plastic bag or a bowl with a plate on top and allow to cool. Peel off the skin using the tip of a small knife. Cut the peppers into quarters and remove the core. Scrape away seeds and discard.

THE CHOP - SIZE GUIDE
All pictures shown are life-size

ROUGHLY CHOPPED PARSLEY

FINELY CHOPPED PARSLEY

DICED TOMATO

DICED CARROT AND CELERY

SLICED ONION

CHOPPED ONION

FINELY CHOPPED ONION

FINELY CHOPPED GARLIC

NOTES FROM THE COOKS ON INGREDIENTS

ANCHOVY FILLETS can be soaked in milk for 10 minutes before using if you find the flavour too pungent. Use ½ tsp of anchovy paste as an alternative to 1 anchovy fillet when called for as an ingredient in a cooked pasta sauce.

BUTTER should always be unsalted when working with the recipes in this book.

CAPERS must be drained before using when they come packed in brine. We prefer to use capers preserved in salt, which are harder to find but worth the effort, since they retain more of their natural flavour than those packed in brine. Capers preserved in salt must be rinsed and dried on paper towels before using.

CHEESES that are most suitable for the pasta pantry are discussed in more detail on page 46. **Fontina** is a semi-soft cheese made from cow's milk with an aromatic flavour and great melting properties. Look for authentic Italian fontina when possible and avoid the more widely available Danish variety. Its name is a derivative of *fondere* – to melt.
Gruyere is a hard Swiss cheese with a sweet, nutty flavour. It melts without becoming oily or rubbery and is a good alternative to fontina cheese.
Parmesan is a hard Italian cheese with a rich, sharp flavour that is nothing like the stale, acrid taste of ready-grated parmesan sold in a tub. Always buy Italian Parmesan. Buy in a piece and grate it as required. See page 46 for further information.
Pecorino Romano is a hard Italian cheese with a tangy, piquant flavour that pairs well with the spicy pasta sauces originating from southern Italy. Use Parmesan as an alternative.
Provolone is a cheese made from cow's milk. It has a light ivory colour, a mild flavour and a smooth texture.

Mascarpone is the creamiest of Italian cheeses. It was originally made as a fresh cheese only in the winter months, and had to be consumed within a couple of days. Now it is manufactured with a UHT process and sold in tubs, allowing it to be a 'long-life' product. It does not have the same superior taste of the highly perishable 'fresh', but is an adequate substitute.
Ricotta is used extensively in Italian cooking. If you can, buy it fresh from authentic Italian delicatessens, but be sure to taste it for freshness before buying and to use it with in 48 hours.

CRUSHED CHILLI FLAKES are a widely available hot seasoning often used as an ingredient in pasta sauces. Referred to as peperoncino in Italian.

DRIED BREADCRUMBS should be made with good white bread that is 2 to 3 days old. Cut the bread into pieces and pulse in a food processor or a blender until reduced to fine crumbs. Spread crumbs on a baking tray and bake in a preheated 150°C (300°F) Gas 2 oven for a 2 to 3 minutes, until dry and crisp. Make a large batch and store in an airtight container for up to 1 month.

EGGS are always large eggs. Recipes made with uncooked egg, such as Carbonara (see page 88) and Cream and Parmesan (see page 49) should not be made for children or elderly persons.

FLOUR for making fresh pasta is ideally Italian pasta flour, **Tipo 00/Doppio Zero** (double zero), which can be found at some supermarkets and in Italian speciality stores. Alternatively, use plain flour. **Semolina** flour is a useful addition when making fresh pasta dough. Sprinkle liberally over freshly made pasta to prevent it from sticking. We recommend buying Italian semolina whenever possible.

GARLIC are always medium-sized cloves unless we indicate otherwise.

LEMONS for lemon zest should be organic whenever possible since they are unwaxed and unsprayed.

MUSHROOMS should never be rinsed in water. To clean mushrooms properly, simply wipe gently with a damp towel. See page 56 for more information on the varieties of mushrooms best suited for pasta.

NUTMEG is sold ground or whole. We recommend buying whole nutmeg and grating it freshly as needed. The flavour of freshly grated nutmeg is vastly superior to anything ground.

PINE NUTS are the most flavourful when they are toasted over medium heat in a dry cast-iron frying pan until golden and fragrant, 5 minutes. Shake the pan frequently. Remove from the pan immediately.

PRAWNS when large should be deveined after removing the shells. Run a small, sharp knife over the top edge of the peeled prawn and rinse away the grit.

PROSCIUTTO is an Italian air-dried, salt cured ham. See page 80 for more information.

OLIVES - see information about the olive varieties best suited for pasta on page 98.

SUN-DRIED TOMATOES are most commonly sold marinated in oil; drain before using. We like to use demi-sec tomatoes that are partly dried and not preserved in olive oil. These must be reconstituted in equal parts vinegar and water for 3 hours. Dry with paper towels and use immediately, or store covered in extra virgin olive oil with 2 or 3 cloves of garlic.

SEA SALT is always preferred in all recipes. Buy it in flakes or crystals. See page 21 for more information.

INDEX

MAIL ORDER SOURCES

UK

THE SHOP AT WEST COUNTRY FINE FOODS
East Farm, Codford St. Mary
Nr. Warminister, Wiltshire BA12 OPJ
T: (01985) 851077
Web site: www.wcf.co.uk
Email: the shop@wcff.co.uk
Pasta flour, fresh wild mushrooms, pancetta, Pecorino and other Italian cheese. Extensive selection of gourmet foods available for mail order.

CARLUCCIO'S
28a Neal Street
London WC2H 9PS
T: 020-7240-1487
F: 020-7497-1361
Specialist Italian ingredients, including pasta flour, capers in salt and Castelluccio lentils.

DIVERTIMENTI
Mail Order Limited
PO Box 6611
London SW15 2WG
T: 020-8246-4300
Catalogue available. Kitchenware, tableware and gourmet ingredients.

TAKE IT FROM HERE
Unit 04
Beta Way
Thorpe Industrial Park
Egham
Surrey
T: 0800 137 064
F: 01784 477 814
Email: martin@donmarinternational.co.uk
Catalogue available. Olive oil, capers in salt, pasta.

Australia

PASTABILITIES
45 Albion Street
Surry Hills, NSW 2010
T: 92810267
F: 92123873

PASTAVERA
186-188 Harris Street
Pyrmont, NSW 2009
T: 96920199
F: 96920917

MYER FOOD HALL
295 Lonsdale St
Melbourne, Victoria 3001
T: (03) 9661 1111

DAVID JONES FOOD HALL
Market Street store
86-108 Castlereagh St
Sydney, NSW 2001
T: (02) 9266 5544
F: (02) 9266 6531

ADELAIDE FRESH PASTA
80b Prospect Rd
Prospect, NSW 5082
T: (08) 8269 3382
F: (08) 8342 1055

THE RE STORE
231 Oxford Street
Leederville, WA 6007
T: (08) 9444 9644

SOMETHING NICE/AUSSIE BASKETS
T: (08) 9383 4053
Email: paola@iinet.net.au

Index compiled by Sue Bosanko

HOW WE MAKE OUR BOOKS

In 1983, a tiny bookstore with a unique concept opened in London's Notting Hill. BOOKS FOR COOKS is a bookstore run by cooks for cooks, selling only cookbooks, teaching cooking classes, cooking from the books and serving up the results in a tiny restaurant among the bookshelves.

I work in the store, cook in the kitchen, and teach in the school. It's true that I acquired my technical training as a professional chef, but to my mind, my real culinary education began the day I crossed the threshold of Books For Cooks. It's from my students and customers that I learn most about the way people live, cook, and eat today, and it's this experience that informs the way we make our books. Real food for real life is our motto. Each title is specially devised to meet the needs of today's busy cooks.

I'm lucky enough to work in a team of dedicated food lovers. We research, test, photograph, write, design, and edit our books from start to finish. All the ingredients are bought from ordinary shops and tested in a domestic kitchen. Our recipes are designed to be cooked at home. Oh yes, and it's all real food in the photographs!

You can write, phone, fax or e-mail us any time.
We'd love to hear from you.

Eric

BOOKS FOR COOKS
4 BLENHEIM CRESCENT
LONDON W11 1NN
TEL: 020-07221-1992
FAX: 020-07221-1517

info@booksforcooks.com

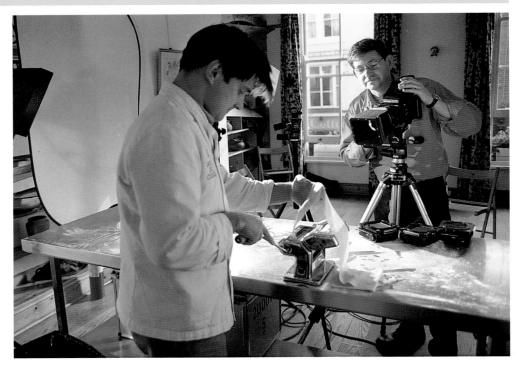